TWICE NO ONE DIES

A K JENKINS

TWICE NO ONE DIES

Wintertime nighs;
But my bereavement-pain
It cannot bring again:
Twice no one dies.

From De Profundis I

– Thomas Hardy

EQUINE PRESS

A.K. Jenkins is an Australian writer who spent many years working in West Africa and Europe before settling in Hobart, Tasmania.

This novel is set in Togo, West Africa in 2004, but the characters and events are entirely fictitious and no resemblance is intended to any event or real person, either living or dead.

Published by Equine Press 2015

Book design and production by Lachlan McLaine
Cover photo by Pierre Gazé

Copyright © Kathryn A Jenkins 2015

National Library of Australia Cataloguing-in-Publication data
   Creator: Jenkins, A. K., author.
   Title: Twice no one dies / A. K. Jenkins.
   ISBN: 9780994260406 (paperback)
   Subjects: Murder--Togo--Fiction.
   Detective and mystery stories.
A823.4

ISBN 978 0 9942604 0 6

for Hannah, Tom and Zoë

1

Lomé, Togo
Friday 12 March 2004

— Get the fuck off the road!

The gendarme was shouting. Aggrieved. He pushed the strap of an AK47 over his shoulder and leaned in the driver's window, bringing with him the reek of alcohol. The gun hit the side of the windscreen with a crack and Marius reminded himself to stay calm.

— You deaf? Get the fuck off the road.

Marius sighed. He couldn't see much in the dark street, but he reversed the old Toyota on to the dirt at the side of the road, turned off his headlights and waited. Behind him other cars were doing the same.

He watched the empty boulevard for signs of movement. No point getting frustrated, nothing he could do. But that hadn't always been the way he felt. A memory floated into his mind – one of those memories like a snapshot, compressed into a single image. It was during his student activist days in Ghana; he was shouting, his right fist raised. The image was silent but he knew what he and the crowd in front of him were shouting. "Power to the people. Power to the people". Then the students would pour out into the streets, following him. It may as well have been war. No sacrifice was too great, that was what he believed. After the coup, after Rawlings and his officers had carried out their executions, "Let the blood flow", he'd shouted to the students and they'd shouted it back.

He wondered what he'd be doing now if he hadn't caught the eye of the new regime in Ghana. It seemed almost overnight that he found himself an Intelligence officer in the Communist Block. New friends, a different life.

In a passive sort of way he'd drifted into making his home here in Togo. After perestroika, he'd been brought back to Ghana then sent as an undercover Intelligence officer to Lomé, working at the university. But the President of Togo was too tough to be blown over by the 'winds of change' sweeping Africa at that time. When being a Ghanaian became too dangerous to keep teaching at the university he'd stayed on here in Lomé. That was when he'd imagined that he and Selina would make a life here together. He pushed that thought away.

Now he'd exhausted both his anger and his idealism. And what else, he wondered. What else have I let go?

He was jolted out of his thoughts by a procession that swept up the boulevard, heading north from the centre of Lomé. As he'd thought, the President.

Marius turned the key to start the engine. Nothing happened. He turned the key again. Still nothing. Behind him cars were pulling back onto the road, their lights sweeping over him. He was going to flood the engine if he kept this up. The only thing was to give it a few minutes. Not the best place to be waiting, but what could he do?

Of course. Why hadn't he thought of it before? He reached down and felt under the front seat until his hand touched a bottle. The cashew brandy. He congratulated himself and leaned down a bit further to pull out the bottle.

— You fucking still here?

The gendarme was back. Marius cursed silently and tried to straighten up but hit his head on the bottom of the steering wheel. Then he felt himself being pulled sideways out of the car.

The first kick got him around the shoulders. He tried to

roll-jump into a standing position but the second kick caught him in the backside and he sprawled forward on his face. Now the rifle butt, Marius thought, but nothing happened and he pushed himself quickly to his feet.

The gendarme was running towards a pick-up truck that had pulled over. Soldiers were crammed around the mounted automatic rifle. He jumped onto the tailboard as it took off again, heading north up the boulevard, away from Lomé.

Marius was suddenly alone in the dark street. He used the back of his hands to brush bits of dirt and gravel off his face. Then he inspected his palms. No blood. He swiped at his clothes and got most of the dirt off.

The front door of the Toyota was hanging open. He climbed in and sat behind the wheel for a minute, breathing slowly. Then he pulled out the brandy, unscrewed the cap and carefully put it in the unused ashtray. He leaned into the sagging back of the driver's seat and made a silent toast. Carpe diem, he thought, and took a mouthful of the cashew brandy. The warmth in his throat and chest was a unique pleasure each time. Another sip, then he replaced the cap and put the bottle back under the seat.

— Okay, old friend, he said to the car. Start now.

He turned the key and rejoiced silently as the engine fired.

When it settled into a steady rhythm he pulled back on to the road. At the intersection he turned left and headed south towards town.

By the time he got to the Peace Roundabout Lomé was back to normal. So was he, more or less. This place, he thought. That was close.

He glanced up at the huge statue of a white dove that rose from a floodlit pedestal in the centre of the roundabout. Part of the olive branch was still hanging from where the dove's mouth used to be, but most of its head had been shot off during what locals called the troubles. Ten years on and it still hadn't been repaired.

A few minutes later Marius made a right turn off the main road. The streets quickly became narrow and dark, the only light coming from the headlamps reflecting off the dirty sand. Every so often he passed a drinking spot lit by kerosene lamps, and the smell of charcoal grilled chicken and yams frying in coconut oil drifted into the car, along with the thump of Afro beat. He breathed it all in through the wide-open car windows and relaxed back in the driver's seat, content.

The turn off he was looking for could be hard to find, even though he'd been going there for years. More like a walking track than a road, he'd almost driven past it when he picked out the handmade sign just visible in the headlights: Le Jazz Spot 200 metres. Tonight someone was selling food right in the entrance to the lane. An odd place to choose, Marius thought. Obviously not someone who owns a car. But he dimmed his lights and waited while some customers pulled stools and tables out of the way to make room for the car. Inching forward, he savoured the smell of grilled fish and gave them a wave of thanks. The lane soon ended at a T-junction with a sprawling sandy road and Marius parked the car next to the ones already there.

He walked across the road and let himself through a wooden gate in the high plaster wall. For a minute he stood just inside the gate, and looked around to see if there was anyone he knew. He had to admit to himself that he was glad to be off the roads.

There were quite a few people here already. They sat in semi-darkness at tables and chairs scattered between low-growing bushes and dim ground lights in a sort of garden. He didn't recognise anyone but then he couldn't see very well in this light. At the far end of the garden the bar was lit by a string of lights that shimmered off the bottles on the shelf at the back. A couple of people were ordering drinks and others were sitting on the high stools.

Midway between where he was and the bar, a neatly thatched roof over a concrete slab served as a bandstand. Marius could see Lucien sitting at the piano and behind him Krupa was unpacking his drum kit. The table directly in front of the band was still empty and Marius headed over to it and sat down. As if that was a signal, the speakers that were strung along the side wall started pumping out the unmistakable sound of Michael Brecker's tenor sax.

Marius was still getting comfortable in his chair and thinking about ordering a drink when Akosua seemed to materialise out of nowhere, as if she'd read his thoughts. Of course, she'd seen him arrive. She was holding a battered tin tray. A bottle of Star beer was lying on it, glass and opener beside it.

— Bon soir Mr Marius.

— Akosua. How good to see you. Still reading my mind, I see.

She laughed and went through her usual routine; the tray laid carefully on the table, the bottle placed upright alongside the glass. Using the chunk of wood with the wide nail driven into the head, she levered the lid off the bottle. Everything took its own time and Marius wondered if Akosua had ever hurried in her life. He took pleasure in watching the operation. The beer tasted better served like this, as if the care, even respect, was an extra ingredient.

Marius watched Akosua. She didn't seem to have changed at all in the years he'd known her. It had been not long after Le Jazz Spot had opened when he'd first met her – it must have been nearly ten years ago. Amazing. It didn't seem so long. The two of them had settled into an exchange that only varied slightly from one visit to the other.

— My dear Akosua. Tell me about your day. Is that husband of yours still jealous of me?

They both glanced across at a table near the bar where Mawuli sat every night. He probably put off some casual drinkers who liked to flirt with waitresses. That and her slight limp perhaps. But Mibou was right to keep her, Marius thought. Reliable, honest, responsible, hardworking. Akosua was all those things and Le Jazz Spot wouldn't be half the place without her.

— Mr Marius, you know he's not like that, she said as usual.

— Well, he should be. A beautiful young woman like you. But really, how are you? How's life?

— What's going to change? She laughed and shook her head.

He knew she had a hard time of it with that jealous husband. Once she'd asked him to help her and he'd done what he could. Mawuli had at least stopped beating her.

Come to that, he knew lots of people's problems. There were a few bars around town that he thought of as his office. It was a hobby of his to analyse people, and he took it as a sort of personal challenge to read their faces and behaviour. Then he'd tease out of them stories about their lives that they wouldn't usually tell anyone. During the years in Intelligence he'd relied on his ability to judge character. The work had finished but he hadn't lost his interest in human nature.

Marius sipped thoughtfully on his beer. That had been too close for comfort, the idiot with the rifle. Now that he gave himself a chance to think about it, he'd been slow on the uptake. Complacent. Never drop your guard. Well, he'd certainly done that, feeling around for the brandy as if he was at home in the living room. The car not starting was the main problem, but he could have been out of the car, bonnet open, looking like he was doing something. Maybe he should think about getting a new car.

He poured some more beer into his glass and shifted the bottle so the condensation didn't drip onto his legs. Friday night at Le Jazz Spot had become a ritual. No matter what else was happening, if he was in Lomé, he was here. The Bou-

Bop band were as good as any in West Africa. Of course they could have their off nights, but by and large he was never disappointed. They played what he thought of as real jazz. God knows what he meant by that. Something very African: rhythm, energy, humour, feeling. Not easy to put your finger on what it was exactly, but he missed it in other places he'd been to.

He felt a tap on his shoulder and turned around. Mibou was standing behind him, a large black leather instrument bag hanging off each shoulder. Mibouré a Bidas – owner of Le Jazz Spot and leader of the Bou-Bop band. Around town he had a reputation for being a bit wild, but Marius knew he was a serious musician.

— Marius. Bon soir. Thinking as usual! Let me buy you another drink. Akosua!

Mibou leaned down to greet Marius and the saxophone in its leather bag swung round and knocked the table. The half empty bottle rocked and was caught by Marius before it could fall.

— My good man. To misquote my friend Diogenes, what I most like to drink is the beer of others. Bring it forth.

— You and your Diogenes! Mibou's Satchmo voice was a low growl.

He gave Marius a friendly slap on the shoulder and wandered over to the bandstand where the others were setting up. Lucien was warming up the old piano, playing a new fifth progression; at the same time he was picking out the keys that weren't working and noting them for later. As Mibou came up he finished with a fast run down the keyboard, continuing into space and faking a near fall off the piano seat. Mibou's whole face broke into a booming laugh and he did his own fake fall, letting himself drop to one side then doing a quick recovery. It wasn't Lucien's style to laugh much, but he gave a lopsided smile and raised his left eyebrow.

7

Marius started on his second beer and watched them. Lucien looked almost normal sitting at the piano. Straight back, powerful wide shoulders, blond shoulder length dreads and a glowing, light brown skin. His eyes were wide set and large with arching eyebrows. If he were female, his nose might be described as pert – unusual for an African. But when he stood up he only came to just above Mibou's waist height. Marius admired the way he got around using a couple of short walking sticks. There were plenty of men in his position wheeling themselves about on trolleys and living by begging. Impossible to imagine Lucien doing that.

Mibou unzipped one of the leather bags and inspected his beloved Selmer Mark VI. With care he attached it to his lanyard and had a blow, adjusted the mouthpiece, tried again. It would do. Just. Time for some new reeds. He went over to the storage area at the back, brought out a stand and placed his sax on it. Then he did the same thing with his guitar, and tested the microphone. Akizi had plugged his bass into the heavy old amplifier and was fiddling with the controls, trying to get rid of the static. Mibou brought out the mixing board then went over to help him.

Marius was on his third beer by the time the band finally kicked off with 'Wonderful World'. Even on this old standard they sounded good. Tight but relaxed, playing around with the improvs, taking the familiar tune into new places. Mibou's gravelly voice suited the song and despite the roughness of his untrained voice, you could feel people being drawn to it.

Konban wa. Ii desuka? Mimi slipped quietly into the chair next to him.

She put a glass of wine and a bottle on the table and Marius noticed she was a bit tipsy. The baggy top and tight jeans she was wearing made her look even tinier than usual, but elegant and pretty.

— All the better for seeing you, he said.

Mimi smiled and took a sip of her wine then leaned towards him.

— I'm going to sing tonight, she whispered.

They sat easily together, both lost in the music. Mimi was the daughter of Marius' great friend Takashi. He'd known her since she came to Togo from Japan as a little girl of eight and she was like a daughter to him. Mimi had gone back to Osaka to university, but she missed her father and had come back a few years ago. She was working as a teacher at the Lomé International Community School.

Mimi thought Marius was looking pretty good. It made her laugh when he called himself an old man. Hardly. Sure, his tightly curled hair was mostly grey as was the stubble and those bushy eyebrows. Maybe he looked a year or two over forty-seven – the age she knew he was. Almost since she'd known him – at least since she'd taken notice – he'd been wearing the same sort of shirts: collarless, light coloured soft cotton, falling from a square yoke. He called it his philosopher's look. It was fine for here in the tropics but if he ever carried out his threat to go to Japan with her and Takashi, he'd need to change his style.

She sensed someone behind her and looked up to see Louis. Much darker than the other musicians, his teeth glowed white in his big smile.

— Louis. Bon soir. Comment? Join us.

Mimi stood up, tiny against Louis, and gave him a big hug. He was a great friend of all of them. A gentle giant, he loved his trumpet above all else; then jazz, women and beer. A Beninoise, he played with the Brassafrique band over there. And over here he taught some high-paying students and jammed wherever he could.

— Where's Lillian? Mimi asked him. She was used to seeing the two of them together at the Spot.

— In Paris. Visiting her son. Here. Can you look after this?

Mimi took the battered looking case and put it on a spare chair. As he walked across to join the band he was already blowing on his trumpet. Marius and Mimi settled back to enjoy the music.

After what happened, Marius kept going back over that night. There was no way he could have known it would be the last time they were all together at Le Jazz Spot, but the signs of tension were there; a jumpy, unpaid, trigger-happy military driven by a President determined to hold on to power no matter what. Trouble was, there had been too many times when it was like that, especially when elections were in the offing. He was kidding himself if he thought there was anything he could have done to prevent it, but he couldn't shake the feeling that he somehow should have been ahead of the game.

2

At 4 o'clock on this Sunday, just like every other Sunday, the main beach in Lomé was packed with families in their Sunday best. Mimi arrived in a taxi with Mibou and Lucien. For most of the day they'd been playing around with some ideas for an album and were ready for a break.

They walked through the shade of the straggling coconut palms and down towards the sea. The sun was hazed out by thick cloud and the air moist and heavy. People were standing in groups talking, or wandering down the beach to watch men and boys pulling in fishing boats on the end of long ropes. The water was the colour of a Ming vase and cloudy in the same way, with a sharp break right at the water's edge. No one was swimming.

Just along from them a man was holding a quiet brown horse by a piece of old rope. Mibou walked over and talked to the man. Mimi could see the man shaking his head but Mibou put a hand on his shoulder and whispered something in his ear. They both laughed and Mibou swung up into the saddle, his sax in its case jolting against the horse. He sat up very straight, his blue and orange shirt, missing a button or two, flapped in the sea breeze. Mimi felt half embarrassed, half amused. She thought that Mibou looked quite at home, and was surprised. He pulled his mobile phone from the leather pouch attached to his belt and held it to his right ear.

— Photo, he called out to her. Take a photo.

Mimi laughed and obliged, using the Pentax she always carried around with her. Mibou was energised for the camera, playing to it in a way that seemed to be second nature.

Mibou used the man's shoulder to help him down off the horse and gave him a few CFA.[1] The three of them strolled down to the edge of the water. Mimi played around in the small waves, sandals in one hand and the skirt of her sundress bundled in the other.

Mibou and Lucien stood watching. Mimi let the warm sea swirl around her ankles and looked back at them. They made a striking pair, she thought. Lucien with his blonde dreads and Mibou with his carefully straightened dark hair pulled in at the nape of his neck. Relaxed, happy. Like all Lucien's friends, she never really noticed his height; he was funny, moody, kind, talented; not handicapped.

Mibou's phone rang.

— Tu est où?

It was Marius.

— At the beach, with Lucien and Mimi.

— Okay. Can you get to Chez Miki? Marius sounded tense.

— Sure. We can walk along the beach. Why? What's up?

— I'll tell you when you get here.

— Is it Takashi?

— No. No…he's fine. Marius hesitated on the other end of the line. It's Louis.

Mimi saw the change of mood and went over to them. Her skirt billowed softly around her.

— Problem?

— Maybe. Marius is with your dad. Something about Louis but he didn't say what.

Lucien had a gig in a couple of hours so he decided to

---

1 CFA (céfa) is the Togolese currency, pronounced like the English word 'safer'.

go into town. Mibou and Mimi made their way through the crowd and headed away from the city. They walked quickly and before long the beach was empty.

— Any ideas? Mimi was the first to break the silence.

— None. Well maybe a moto-taxi accident, that sort of thing. But why would Marius be so mysterious?

— Perhaps Lillian's husband beat him up. Mimi was only half joking. Everyone knew about Louis and Lillian, yet Philippe, her husband, seemed to dote on her. Mimi had only met him once – at the party he threw for Lillian's fiftieth birthday – and she found him unsettling. He acted as if everyone was his best friend, but she could sense that he was really aloof from them, as if it was more a business he was running than a party. And all those sentimental speeches!

The sun was getting low in the sky, turning into an orange ball, taking some of the heat with it. Crabs made little openings in the sand as the waves receded. Occasionally they saw farmers digging in the market gardens that ran between the beach and the road.

After twenty minutes or so a slatted walkway half covered in drifted sand marked the beginning of Chez Miki, Takashi's beach bar and restaurant. It was named after his wife Miki, Mimi's mother. She'd been killed by a crazed admirer while singing in their jazz bar in Osaka. Takashi wanted to get as far away from Japan as he could so he'd sold up everything and brought Mimi here to Togo. He'd started a drumming centre first, then a beach bar and then a restaurant. And he'd built a house, made a home, become part of the community. Twenty years on and Chez Miki was a Lomé fixture.

Near the water's edge a Togolese family was packing up bamboo beach mats. The two children, glistening and dark, were running in and out of the waves. Further up the beach in the bar a bored looking waitress was serving beer to a group of Europeans. Mimi waved to her and led the way around the bar and up the walkway to the back entrance of their house. The high wall was plastered a dusky rose colour and in places was almost covered by orange and purple bougainvillea. A heavy wooden gate opened into the garden.

Takashi and Marius were sitting around the wooden table in the palm thatched palava hut. Little paths and terracotta pots were placed among carefully shaped trees and shrubs. Between the glass wall of the house and the garden, rocks and a stone bridge suggested a watercourse. Mimi could see from her father's face that something was wrong; there was a hint of tension in the corners of his mouth. No one else would notice – his friends here joked all the time about his inscrutable poker face.

Mibou pointed to the mugs of beer on the table and sat down in one of the cane chairs.

— Any more where that came from?

Mimi sat and waited until Takashi had organised the beers. She leaned back in the chair, beer in hand, and looked first at her father, then at Marius.

— Okay. What's happened?

Marius was the one to speak.

— There's no easy way to put this. Louis's dead. He was attacked with a machete and left on the beach not far from here. His body was found this morning.

The late afternoon breeze dropped suddenly and the stillness in the garden seemed to intensify the noise of the cicadas. Scent from jasmine hung in the air and somewhere close by a voodoo drum was beating.

Mibou felt his stomach drop and his mouth seemed sucked dry. Nobody spoke. He gulped down most of his beer in one go to fill the hole that seemed to have opened up inside him.

— But I was playing with him on Friday night. He was in top form. Who would want to kill Louis? You know his real name is Parfait and we always tease – teased – him: Parfait by

14

name, Parfait by nature. It doesn't make any sense.

— Well, whoever killed him, it's probably not who our friends the gendarmerie would have us think. Marius looked at Takashi, who raised his beer mug in his direction.

— Please, go ahead.

Marius' Ewé accented French could be hard to follow and the others drew closer to him. He glanced around the garden and dropped his voice.

— This is more or less how it goes. Takashi was minding his own business this afternoon when a group of military chaps came to sample the beer. He bought the first round and made sure there were plenty of reasons for keeping within hearing distance. There was one thing that they kept talking about – some chap whose body was found on the beach not far from the border. It would seem this poor fellow had been taken to with a machete while engaging in some sort of drug deal. They talked about plastic packets of cocaine in the pockets of his jeans. And they weren't surprised because this fellow was a musician and everyone knows they're all on drugs and can't be trusted. Some trumpeter fellow – even called himself that on his carte d'identite – a Beninoise. Name of Parfait Badarou. So Takashi rang me once they finally left and I checked with my friend at the border station. Confirmed.

He stopped talking and slowly sipped his beer.

— What sort of story is that? Mibou muttered. Everyone knows that Louis never touched drugs. And why would he go to that beach at night? Or anywhere along the beach, let alone that spot. Nothing makes sense – there's something wrong.

— If it smells like a rat…. Takashi didn't have to finish the sentence. He glanced at the almost empty glasses, called Yao over and ordered another round of drinks.

— Did they say who killed him? Mimi felt strange asking such a practical question about something that still seemed like a script for a film.

— No. No name. They were talking about drug dealers
– the gangs that operate across the border. Of course they
blamed the Nigerians. It's always the Nigerians. Now he was
being sarcastic. But for sure it's the way those gangs operate,
and they leave the bodies around as a warning for people. But
you're right Mibou. Neither Takashi nor I can swallow that
story. As Takashi says, there's a strong smell of a rat.

Yao put the tray of beer mugs on the table next to
Takashi. The mugs, straight out of the freezer were frosted
white. He went around clockwise removing the empty mugs
and replacing them with full ones. Then he gave the table a
good wipe, picked up the tray and walked carefully across the
little stone bridge and into the house. Around them the drums
filled the silence.

— Who do you think it was if it wasn't drug dealers? Mimi
asked the question that they were all thinking.

Marius shrugged and lifted his hands.

— No idea. Well okay, a couple of ideas, but nothing
definite.

Mibou thought about the comment Mimi had made when
they were walking along the beach – that birthday party
for Lillian, with Philippe pretending to enjoy himself and
playing the good host and husband. Mibou could remember
part of the little speech that Philippe had made. He'd been
standing with his chair pushed back from the table, Lillian
sitting down next to him, her head turned up, smiling at him.
Philippe had gazed down at her, one hand gently resting on
her right shoulder, the other holding the microphone. He'd
asked them to fill their glasses with champagne and drink to
his darling Lillian, "who means everything in the world to
me". And he'd asked the band to play 'There will never be
another you'.

As Mibou led off with the melody on his sax, he had
watched Philippe and Lillian on the dance floor. He held her

16

close, dancing as if in a dance class: very formal and upright, one hand holding Lillian loosely around the waist, the other holding her hand tucked in against his chest. Mibou had seen Louis watching them, sipping on a beer, his face not showing any expression at all. He'd found it strange and a bit menacing in a way that he couldn't quite pin down. Now with Louis dead, Mibou wondered if Philippe had organised the party, his speech, the music, as a message to Lillian and Louis. In some ways it made more sense than Philippe's pretense to be blind to what was going on under his nose.

He shared his thoughts with the others. Only Marius had any background on Philippe de Brujin, a Dutchman dealing in African antiques. Rumours went around about his ruthlessness, his possible connections with some of the shadowy business dealings in Lomé, even that his antique dealing was a front for gun running which was how he'd managed to live in such a mansion, drive his new model Mercedes. But they were just rumours – nothing more.

— He's worth checking out. There's something not quite right about Philippe de Brujin. But is he dangerous? Could he kill Louis, or get someone else to, even if he wanted him out of the way? And if it wasn't him, then who and why?

Marius let them think about it. He picked up his beer mug to have a drink, then had a closer look. A small black fly was struggling in the froth. He carefully tilted his mug away from him and flicked the fly expertly with a finger and thumb. Some of the froth went with the fly and they both landed on the edge of the table. Marius and the others watched the fly for a minute or so while it frantically beat its wings, gradually freeing itself of the sticky foam. It dragged itself across the table towards Mimi. She poked it gently with a long nail and suddenly it flew off.

No one had an answer to his questions so Marius spelled it out for them.

— There's something going on here that we all find odd and sinister. So what do we do? We can't just front up to a police station and complain! This isn't some nice 'home of the free' country. It's Togo, where Le Crocodile[2] has his filthy hands in everything. Him and that joke of a justice minister. Justice! Between them, they can do whatever they like.

— You're right Marius, Mimi said. The intimidation is worse than usual with these elections coming up. Some of the drivers bringing kids to school have been dragged out of their cars and beaten. For nothing. It doesn't matter if you stay out of politics. I think they're trying to make us all too scared to go outside. As if we have a choice!

Takashi nodded his agreement.

— And it's been worse since those opposition marches. The only opposition that the Crocodile will allow is the one that he controls.

Marius settled back into the soft floral cushion. He looked thoughtfully at each of them in turn.

— So…the question remains. What can we do? Should we even think of doing anything? We can just let it drop. Almost certainly that's what we should do.

But he was thinking of Louis, good friend, fine musician. He might have lost his old zeal for reform, but there were some things still worth sticking your neck out for. He couldn't just let it go. Justice would be good, but even to dignify Louis' death with the truth would count for something. Nobody said anything. Mibou shook his head slowly from side to side and they knew what he meant. What could they do?

Marius leaned both elbows on the table and cupped his chin in his hands. Night had fallen and the air was still and soft. It was getting hard to see in the dark and the break and sigh of waves sounded close, as if the sea was just the other side of the

---

1 *Le Crocodile* was a name commonly used to refer to the President of Togo.

fence. The perfume of the jasmine was stronger now.

— Okay. Here's what I think. I think I owe it to Louis to clear his name and find the killer. Or killers. But it's not a game. Mimi's right. The random violence is getting worse.

He told them about Friday night and his brush with the gendarme.

— And, he added, that's just the visible intimidation. Never underestimate the level of surveillance that goes on in this place. You have to assume that someone is listening in on all your phone calls. They mightn't be, but then again they might. Same with emails. And don't tell anyone else what we're doing. This has to stay just between us. I really mean No one else, even people you think you can trust.

They seemed stunned into silence and Marius decided not to share with them what he was about to say, which was that already there were too many of them; too many possibilities for a slip up. At least his point had gone home. Time to change the subject.

— Oh, and one more thing. I was thinking about Lillian. She probably has no idea about any of this. An image of Lillian floated into his mind. A plump bottle blond with a loud infectious laugh, he hated to think just how terrible the news was going to be for her.

— You're right. She's in Paris. Who's going to tell her? Mibou's gravelly voice was even deeper than usual.

They all looked at him and he got the message.

— Okay, okay, I'll do it.

— Thanks Mibou. Marius was relieved to have that one taken off his shoulders. You know her better than the rest of us. I'll see what I can find out about Philippe. Mimi, Takashi, keep your ears open. Something happened on the beach not far from here and you know how it is – there's probably someone who saw it. You've got pretty good links with the people around here.

Mimi stood up and reached across for the tray. She pulled it close then loaded the empty glasses and bottles on to it. She might be a teacher now, but the habits picked up from years of helping out in Chez Miki were part of her. Mibou helped her with the last of the glasses

Inside Chez Miki a group of German tourists had just arrived and Takashi took charge, leading them over to the table with the best view of the softly lit garden. Mibou put the glasses on the bar and he and Marius headed outside. Mimi went to see them off and stood with them in the darkness by the side of the road as they tried to flag down a taxi from the traffic that poured past on the coast road. It didn't take too long. Marius gave her a big hug before he climbed in after Mibou. Mimi watched the taxi merging into the stream of cars then slowly walked back to the restaurant.

3

Mibou paid the taxi driver and crossed the road to his house. Coconut palms rustled softly. Where the dry fronds touched the high wall they made a faint scraping sound like a small animal. He let himself through a carved wooden gate and closed it behind him. It was a relief to be back in his own place. To his right on the other side of the wall was Le Jazz Spot. He could just make out the music playing over the loud speakers – Akosua's favourite, St Germaine. He smiled to himself. She only put it on when he wasn't there. He would usually call in to the bar to make sure everything was okay, but it was the last thing he felt like doing right now. Here it was calm and private; the only light came from a half moon and the darkness suited Mibou. His mind was on Lillian and Louis.

This place, the house and the jazz bar, was his now and he lived here by himself. Had done for – what was it – two and a half years now. It was Françoise who had bought it. After the troubles in the early 1990s, lots of the Europeans had left Togo but she stayed. Aid dried up. Hotels closed. Tourists stopped coming. House prices dropped to next to nothing so she bought this. She was working for the UN and he thought she would make Lomé her home. They'd lived together here for nearly ten years. He still couldn't understand why she'd left, but life goes on. Now he had Antoinette who came on weekdays and organised everything – food, cleaning, gardeners. Easier in some ways. In lots of ways. But he still missed Françoise.

He walked to the house along the path under the old almond tree. Some nuts had fallen from the wide spreading branches and made the ground uneven. He kicked a few aside. Louis had been here with him just a few days ago. They'd carried the bamboo table and chairs from the front patio and set themselves up under the tree; shared a few bottles of beer and gathered the almonds, cracking them open with a couple of rocks and eating the nuts, small but tasty. The table and chairs were still there. Mibou let himself into the house, switched on the light and went to the fridge. He took out a bottle of Star and an iced glass from the freezer and went back out to the almond tree. Paris was two hours ahead of Lomé time so it would already be around 10 pm there. He knew he had to ring Lillian soon. She was a night owl but even so…

He drank the glass of beer quickly and filled it up with the rest of the bottle. Bad news, he thought, bad news. I'll start with that. Nothing was going to make this easy. He picked up his mobile from the table, found Lillian's number and called.

Her phone rang. And rang. Mibou was almost relieved. He wouldn't have to talk to her after all. Then she was on the line.

— Bonsoir. 'Ello.

— Lillian, c'est Mibou.

— Mibou! Tu est ou? Of course she was surprised.

— Lomé. Chez moi. Can you ring me back? He knew that Lillian used some cheap way of ringing on the internet and his credit would only last another minute, if that.

— Bien sur. But is there a problem?

— Yes. Well not exactly. Some bad news. Very bad.

He ended the call just before it cut out. Waited. His eyes were used to the dark now. Behind him he heard the soft thump of an almond hitting the ground.

The phone rang. He let it ring a couple of times, took a deep breath and pressed the button.

— Ciao Lillian.

— Mibou. Is everything okay? You sound a bit bizarre.

— No – things aren't okay. I have really bad news.

— What's happened?

— Something very bad. Mibou couldn't bring himself to say the words. I don't know how to say this Lillian.

— Just say it. Tell me.

— It's Louis. He's…been killed.

There was silence on the other end of the line. Mibou could hear a fridge opening, the clink of glass on a hard surface.

— I'm sorry. I was just getting myself a glass of wine. I can't take it in. Are you telling me that someone killed Louis?

— That's it.

— Who?

— We don't really know. The gendarmes say it was something to do with drug dealing. His body was found on the beach near Agkamé. But we don't believe them.

— When was he killed? I was talking to him on the phone yesterday afternoon and he was going for a drink with some friends. It was just before the news here when we were talking so it must have been about 5 o'clock in Lomé.

— They say he was killed late on Saturday night.

— We were cut off while we were talking. I tried to ring back but the line had dropped out and the phone was dead. Mibou. Listen to me. I can't take this in. I'm going to hang up in a minute. Is there anything else you can tell me?

Mibou didn't know what to say. He kept it simple.

— The police say he had cocaine in his pockets and it was a drug killing. Marius and Takashi don't believe them and I don't either. Louis never used drugs. We all know that but we don't know what to do. Who else would want to kill Louis?

— How was he killed?

— We don't know anything much.

He didn't want to mention the machete and he couldn't say her husband might be one of the suspects. He wondered if that thought would occur to her.

— Mibou. My son's just arrived. I'm going to hang up now. Keep me posted. And merci.

Mibou finished the call and sat very still, holding the phone against his chest as if he could get some comfort from it. Tears ran down his face and he wiped them away with his sleeve. He thought of Friday night – only a couple of days ago – when he and Louis had played together at Le Jazz Spot. Louis was so relaxed and happy. His cheeks were round anyway and playing the trumpet they puffed out as if there were little coconuts in each one. They'd played around with some new riffs, challenging each other. Mibou could tell Louis had been doing some serious practice. But what was the point of all that if you ended up being killed on some dark, lonely beach?

Mibou stood up and took some deep breaths of the night air. He'd go crazy if he kept thinking like that. He grabbed the empty beer bottle and the glass and headed back into the house. A few minutes later he was back with his sax. He attached the mouthpiece and licked the reed. It wasn't exactly right but the slightly flat tone suited his mood. He thought of a song the two of them had played around with for years; 'St Louis Blues' – Louis' signature tune. The almond tree spread above him, trapping the sound, and the soft air seemed to hold the notes in the dark garden. He played it over and over, the improvs getting more and more complex.

When he finally stopped and put his sax on the table he felt better. So what if he died tomorrow. He zipped the sax into its bag and went inside, rinsed his beer glass and put it on the sink. Then he put on the ceiling fan, undressed and sprawled on his bed. In a few minutes he was asleep.

4

Takashi walked down the slatted path to the beach. Where the wooden boards disappeared into the sand he stopped and threw his towel onto the old driftwood log. He kicked off his sandals and felt the sand squeaking under his feet. It was 7.00am. The sun was already warm, but not too hot. He walked down to where the ebbing tide had left the sand moist and firm. This morning hardly a ripple broke the surface of the sea green water in the lagoon, but there was a gentle swell caused by the waves that broke further out against the mostly submerged rocks that had once been the coast road.

He breathed deeply and felt the coolness of the sand under his feet. With a concentrated graceful movement he planted his feet and stretched both hands in front, watching them intently, and began the controlled movements of his t'ai chi routine. It was a discipline that got him through each day.

His t'ai chi finished, he walked slowly into the water and started his daily swim, up and down the lagoon, following the line of the beach. Half an hour later he was towelling himself dry under the shade of the coconut palms that lined the beach. He felt energised and wondered why he always had such a struggle with himself to get up and do this every morning. Holding one corner of the towel in his right hand he flicked it behind his back and caught it with his left. He enjoyed the pull of the towel across his back and closed his eyes, feeling the warmth of the sun against his eyelids.

When he opened them a few seconds later his friend Kwame from the village along the beach was sitting on the log, his legs stretched out in front of him. He was leaning comfortably on his elbows, his back resting against the forked branch as if it was a padded armchair. In dark glasses, a grey singlet top and pink shorts, Kwame looked more like a beach vendor than the owner of a thriving refrigerator repair business. He reached up a hand in greeting and they went through the usual grip-changing ritual, finishing with a sharp snap. Takashi tucked his towel around his waist and sat on the log next to Kwame.

— I heard about Louis. I'm sorry. Kwame spoke in French with the sharp twang of the Mina people. His father had been a fisherman and Kwame was the only one in his family to make a break with that tradition.

— Thank you. Takashi waited. Neither of them wasted time with words but there was an understanding between them. They'd been friends for nearly twenty years. Takashi still wondered how he would ever – and if he would ever – have started Chez Miki without Kwame there to save him from the worst of the traps that foreigners in Togo are apt to fall into. Buying a freezer that turned out not to work from a self-appointed friend who charged twice the going rate was one of the first things that went wrong. Luckily for Takashi, it was Kwame who had fixed it with his usual mix of ingenuity and know-how.

— I heard it was 'the beach boys'. Kwame used the name the locals called the small time drug dealers that traded cocaine across the Ghanaian border.

— That's what the police are saying.

— You don't believe them?

— No. I don't know what's going on but that wasn't Louis' thing. Jazz, beer, women. Not drugs.

— Another terrible thing has happened. Do you know the Atsou family?

— Sure. Kweku and his boat La Danse de la Mer – I buy fish from him when he gets a good catch.

— His son Kodjo was shot on Saturday night. He's dead.

Takashi looked at Kwame then back out to sea. The sun was sending sparks off the water. Foam shone white beyond the lagoon and closer in the blue-green water lay still and inviting. The gentle swells sent occasional ripples up the beach. It all looked calm and beautiful, like paradise. But there was something very ugly going on here. He turned back to Kwame.

— Is that Kweku's eldest?

— No. It's his second son. Then there are the two girls.

— Do you know what happened?

— Not really. It looks like Kodjo went out to have a pee during the night and was shot. From quite a way off Kweku said. It must have been the military police with that sort of gun. You know they do that sometimes – to intimidate. Or just for fun. Who knows? Maybe they were drunk.

— Where was he exactly?

— Do you know where their hut is?

— Vaguely. Takashi pictured the shantytown that was Agkamé village. A dirt track wound through a maze of palm thatch and corrugated iron huts. The sand on the track had been gouged into deep holes in the heavy downpours so he usually walked there when he wanted to organise some fish. He'd always met Kweku at the simple bamboo and palm structure that was the drinking spot for that part of the village. With good-humoured irony the locals called it The Ritz.

— Their hut's between The Ritz and the beach. Kodjo was found just near the bar in a stand of palms, not far off the road. Why?

— Just wondering. It's odd. When was he shot?

— Looks like it was some time during Saturday night – probably in the early hours of the morning. Kwame leaned forward and rested his elbows on his knees, turning his head to look at Takashi.

— Even odder.

— Same night as Louis?

— Yep. Same night. And not far away. The police claim they found Louis on the beach just down from the sea wall where the boats tie up. That can't be more than a kilometre or so from the Ritz.

The two men exchanged glances. Kwame took his sunglasses off and rubbed his fingers over his eyes. There were thoughts that didn't need saying. Distrust and fear of the government and the military ran very deep. There was nothing they wouldn't do – everyone knew that.

Takashi looked back at the sea, still green and sparkling.

— Louis was killed with a machete, he said. They found bags of cocaine in his pockets.

Kwame put his glasses back on and holding them with one hand he looked over the rim at Takashi, his eyebrows raised.

— And yet…was all he said.

They stood and walked down to the water's edge, both lost in thought.

— And yet…echoed Takashi. He didn't really have any clear thoughts, just the knowledge that something was very wrong.

— I'll let you know if I hear anything else, Kwame said. He rested his hand lightly on Takashi's shoulder then turned and walked back down the beach back towards Agkamé.

Takashi nodded his thanks and slowly headed back to his house, re-tying the towel around his waist as he walked. He was thinking about what Kwame had just told him. Was Kodjo's death just a coincidence? If there was a connection between the murder of Louis and the murder of Kodjo, what could it possibly be? They didn't know each other. It definitely wouldn't be Philippe because he would have no reason to kill

Kodjo. If only they could find out more about how Louis was killed.

Then he had sudden thought. What if Louis was shot too? Shot and then attacked with a machete? Maybe the machete was used to cover up the shooting. If only it were possible to see his body. Maybe Marius would have some ideas – he usually did.

5

There was still heavy dew on the grass when Marius pushed open the French windows and let himself on to the terrace. He had to lift and push at the same time to stop the doors scraping on the chipped black and white tiles, but despite the rather battered look, he loved the faded glory of the old house. The weathered shutters and long windows gave it a Venetian look, and inside the high ceilings with their slow moving fans brought to mind colonial days. There was something rather ironic that appealed to him about living here. Maybe not irony exactly, but from what he knew, the earlier occupants – European bureaucrats – would have been appalled to think of a 'native' living in such a place.

He pulled his favourite old cane chair closer to a little glass table, put down his mug of ginger tea and settled back to enjoy the still fresh morning. Some people thought it was a bit odd that he still lived in the house. After all, it had belonged to Selina's family and still did, for that matter. Selina. It was four years since she'd died. March 15, the ides of March. Maybe that's why he was thinking about her more than usual. Or it could be that Louis' sudden death had brought it all back.

It still seemed impossible. Of course they'd talked about her being a sickler[1] before they got married, but his blood

---

1 A *sickler* is a person who has an inherited disorder of the haemoglobin that affects the red blood cell function.

group was AA, so the problem wouldn't be passed on to children, and it seemed such a small thing at the time. And really it was. Most of the time she was fine. Then some rare complication happened out of the blue and a few days later she was dead.

There were quite a few people he knew – none of them close friends though – who couldn't understand why he didn't just move on, get another wife, have more children. There'd been plenty of attempts at matchmaking, some of it obvious, some less so. He'd tried to take it with good humour, but his heart just wasn't in it. Thank goodness they'd all given up now, though he could see their point of view and he knew better than to say 'never'.

Four years. In one way it had gone quickly. Dzigi had been six when Selina died and keeping life reasonably normal for him was his first priority. It was just lucky timing that Selina's sister Eva and her daughter Seri were between houses, and it suited all of them for her to stay with Marius and help out. Seri was a couple of years older than Dzigi, but they got on pretty well and before they knew it a year had gone, then two. The arrangement worked so well it had become permanent without either of them really making a decision. Marius could easily see why people found it odd; two unmarried in-laws living together like this. But the house was big enough for them each to have a wing to themselves and it worked. Neither of them had any plans to change it in the short-term at least.

There were times when he allowed himself to recognise that he also liked the house because it was part of the fabric of his relationship with Selina and living here with her sister kept some sort of connection with her. So strange. Everything he did with Selina had seemed so easy. Strange because he'd resisted being tied down and completely rejected the idea of living with one's in-laws; laughed at friends who got themselves into that situation. Yet when he'd married Selina, her mother and father had been living here in this house and for a couple of years they'd all lived here together and even that worked pretty well. The arrangement only ended when her father's company sent him to work in France.

In the months after Selina died it was Dzigi who told Marius how to do everything. Mummy did it this way. Marius understood his need to keep things as much the same as usual, so he learned the routine. Now it was second nature, but what was it about leaving for school that brought things so close to chaos? The homework, the lunch, the snack, the uniform, the sports kit, the excursion. There was always something.

When Marius wasn't away working the best part of the day was just after they all left for school and work, like now. He looked at his watch. It was still only 7.30. What about that promise he'd made last night? Without thinking too much, he'd offered to check up on Philippe de Brujin. Just how was he going to do that?

There was definitely some pretty unhealthy competition – sometimes violence – in parts of the artifacts trade. In a way it wasn't too different from trading drugs or arms. And if Philippe wanted to use someone else to get rid of Louis he had the connections.

But more to the point, what did Philippe really think about Louis and Lillian? The reality was that he probably didn't see Louis as being worth noticing at all. Philippe was definitely not one to put himself on the same level as us, thought Marius. Louis probably counted as less than nothing; just some black guy who hung around bars playing the trumpet. Marius knew that Philippe didn't share Lillian's love of jazz. So if Louis didn't count, why make the effort to get rid of him? On the other hand, Philippe's sentimental displays towards Lillian might be a cover. The truth might be that he was jealous of the good-looking musician. Marius didn't consider himself much of a judge of appearances, especially of Europeans, but even he could see that Philippe came off second best when it came to looks, with his narrow round shoulders, pendulous stomach and red face. Still, he was pretty typical of a group of such men here in Lomé and their arrogance suggested that they were pleased enough with themselves and sure that money and influence made up for everything.

Marius realised he wasn't getting anywhere. He was usually confident in his judgment of people but he couldn't make up his mind. On balance he thought it unlikely that Philippe would bother to get his hands dirty by killing Louis, but that wasn't good enough. He got up and wandered across the rough lawn to the carved totem under the trees. It was taller than he was and he looked up at the staring eyes in the rigid wooden face. That usually helped when he needed an idea.

It didn't fail him now. As he ran his hand over the smooth wood and admired the carving, a plan started to emerge. Artifacts. That was it. He pulled out his mobile and dialled the number of his friend Jean-Pierre, owner of the Tribal Gallery in town and an honest collector of African art. Sure – he could arrange a meeting between Philippe and Marius. If Marius was looking for a mask from Benin, then Philippe was quite the expert on those. How about 3 o'clock this afternoon at Les Palmes?

— Perfect, Marius said.

As he was putting his phone back in his pocket he heard the familiar whine of the old Toyota and Jojo negotiated the narrow entrance to the driveway and pulled up in front of the garage. One of these days I must get that shed cleaned out, Marius thought. It wasn't a new idea but he could never seem to find the motivation to get started.

It was Jojo who mostly drove the kids to school in the morning and usually he'd pick them up again in the afternoon. Marius watched him as he filled up a bucket of water and started washing the car with the same intensity that he gave to everything he did. What a contrast with the aimless young Jojo Marius had taken into the household ten years ago. Now he was more like a trusted friend than an employee. One-man-thousand they all called him because he seemed to be able to fix anything: machines, problems.

Marius strolled over and stood out of the range of the water that Jojo was splashing on to the car. He had an idea. Jojo often talked about his cousins who lived in Lomé – he seemed to spend all his spare time visiting one or the other of them. Marius could never really work out the complicated web of these relatives, but he thought he could remember Jojo saying something about a cousin who worked at Philippe and Lillian's house.

It also occurred to Marius that he really needed some help with – what was it? An investigation? Project? Mission? Anyway, even though there were already too many of them involved in this search for Louis' killer, he knew that sooner rather than later he'd need someone who could do some leg work without being noticed. Jojo was perfect. He seemed to be related to every second person in Lomé and Marius trusted him completely.

Marius took his time and explained everything. Jojo didn't say much. Every so often he went over to the tap next to the garage and refilled the bucket with water. Once or twice Jojo asked a question, but he didn't seem at all surprised and Marius had the impression that he had already had some idea as to what was going on. How that could be the case he had no idea, but it made things easier.

He finished by explaining about the arrangement he'd just made to meet up with his friend Jean-Pierre and Philippe de Brujin at Les Palmes and he asked Jojo about his cousin. Yes, Kofi was one of the security guards at the de Brujin's place. Les Palmes was right across from the de Brujin's house, so while Marius was at the meeting he could call in and chat to him about things, ask about Saturday night. But who would pick up Dzigi and Seri after school? Marius gave Eva a ring. As it turned out it wasn't too much of a problem for her to do the school run this afternoon.

So at 3.00pm sharp Jojo pulled to the side of a potholed road and parked the old Toyota against the wall of Philippe de Brujin's house, carefully pulling into the scant shade of a couple of old palm trees. Marius wandered across to Les Palmes, a cross between a pension and a hotel. Jojo gave Kofi a call on his mobile and shortly afterwards he heard the rattle of a chain being lifted and his cousin let him into the courtyard of the de Brujin house.

Inside the whitewashed walls of Les Palmes a vine covered trellis and spreading trees shaded a tiled courtyard. The courtyard was linked to the bar by a deep loggia and Marius felt as if he could be in the Mediterranean somewhere. He was glad of the coolness; this time of the afternoon was only bearable in the rainy season and that was still a few months away.

He stopped just inside the gate and looked around. His eyes took a few seconds to adjust to the shade and then he noticed a hand waving. Jean-Pierre and Philippe were over to his left, the only customers sitting under the trellis.

They both stood up as he neared the table. Jean-Pierre, elegant and cool looking as usual, greeted him enthusiastically, kissing him on both cheeks. Philippe held out his hand and Jean-Pierre did the introductions. Marius was relieved that Philippe didn't remember seeing him at Lillian's 50th – the house had been crowded and they'd never been introduced so he wasn't surprised. He'd been there with Mibou and Lucien and right now he would rather Philippe didn't know about that friendship.

Three large bottles of Star and two hours later the three of them left Les Palmes together. Marius hoped he wouldn't have to buy the voodoo mask that had been the pretext for the meeting. Philippe was an expert on them, Jean-Pierre the link. But if he had to, he wouldn't mind if he could get it down to a reasonable price. He liked the masks from Ouidah and there was that gap on his library wall he'd been meaning to fill for years now.

They said their goodbyes just near the Toyota and Marius was relieved to see Jojo back in the car. Not that it would seem odd for Jojo to look up his cousin and spend time gossiping but still, Marius just felt happier that Philippe knew as little as possible about both of them.

He let himself into the passenger's seat and Jojo started the car. The plan was to continue out to Chez Miki to talk to Takashi. Mibou and Lucien would be there too and Marius was anxious to find out what Lillian had said to Mibou. It would all be so much easier if they could use their phones, but the risk was just too great. Surveillance was a problem at the best of times and this wasn't one of those. Only a few weeks to the election and there were some grim stories going around about interrogations that could only have been because of phone taps. Even if only half of them were true, that was too many.

Jojo carefully put the car into first gear and pulled slowly into the wide sandy street. He drove sedately, weaving around the gouged holes in the road.

— So. What did you find out? Marius asked.

— A little bit. Kofi was the security guard on Saturday night.

Jojo spoke in Ewé and Marius switched from French to his native tongue. It felt good. Marius waited. Jojo always chose his words with deliberation.

— The boss went out in the Audi soon after dark. He got home late – just after two. Jojo slowed the car almost to a halt and let it drop into a water filled hollow that took up most of the road. Back on the packed sand he continued. My cousin's pretty sure of the time. He'd been in big trouble for falling asleep so he was taking a walk every half hour and checking the clock.

— Did he notice what the boss was wearing?

— Like he was going out somewhere a bit special – the white trousers and jacket.

—Anything else? Did he talk about madame and Louis?

— He thinks the boss is too much in love with madame. That he should be more stronger. Maybe stop madame going out by herself.

— Thanks Jojo.

They drove in silence. Marius went over what he'd found out. When he'd dropped the ghastly details of Louis' death into the conversation, Philippe seemed genuinely shocked and surprised. Of course he could have been pretending but Marius' gut feeling was to believe him. That was really all Marius had expected to get from the carefully planned meeting. To take Philippe unawares with the blunt facts and to observe. He felt sure that Lillian wouldn't have rung him to pass on the news.

There seemed to be unwritten boundaries around Lillian's friendship with Louis, boundaries that enabled both of them to pretend; to know and not know. Marius could see the hypocrisy but thought that on balance it worked rather well. It wasn't his style but he couldn't get worked up about it.

According to Jojo's cousin, Philippe had been wearing smart white trousers and a jacket. That didn't fit well with a murder. It was more the sort of thing he'd be likely to wear to one of those poolside parties that the well-heeled here liked so much. Of course there was always the possibility that the murder was contracted out by Philippe de Brujin and then he could have a perfect alibi if he was in fact at a pool party.

Again, Marius couldn't seem to get a picture in his head of de Brujin as a killer. Should he just go with his intuition? But from what Jojo had told him, Philippe couldn't be ruled out. He hadn't got home until after two and he'd taken the car. He could have hired someone else to do the murder and they might have used the car. Marius was still going round in circles; all questions and no answers. And here was another one. When had Louis really been killed and how was he going to find that out?

They were heading out of Lomé along the Boulevard de la République, the Gulf of Guinea on the right and the sun setting behind them. Marius wound the window down and let the sea wind blow into his face. There was no point going over and over the same thing. He took a couple of sips from the bottle of cashew brandy that he kept in the car and settled back to enjoy the drive.

6

Half an hour later they pulled off the road on to the gravel in front of Chez Miki. Jojo turned off the engine and the Toyota spluttered, shook, and fell silent. Marius took one last swig from the brandy bottle then screwed the cap back on and put it under his seat.

While they were on the road night had fallen and the entrance to Chez Miki was lit by a string of red and black Japanese lanterns hung over the slatted wooden doors. To the right of the entrance, water from a bamboo pipe trickled gently into a huge African pot. On the left a cluster of three drums rested against the wall. They were twisted with rough black twine and decorated with ochre and black triangles. Neat stands of bamboo were planted between flat granite rocks and gave the illusion of stepping-stones. Marius always felt an ineffable pleasure as he crossed the stones, as if he was walking into a different world. Anyway, it was a contrast to the stinking noisy traffic and the rough potholed road behind him.

He slid open the door and stepped on to the polished wood floor. Above him a soaring thatched roof was lined with wood panelling and supported by thick pillars and cross beams. Carefully placed shoji screens and Japanese style floor lamps made from rice paper and bamboo created semi-private areas and gave a warm glow to the whole space.

The first person Marius saw was Takashi. He was standing

at the head of a long table proposing a toast to a group of people Marius recognised as drumming students. Takashi acknowledged him with a slight lift of his wine glass, but kept on talking. He had a blue and white band of cotton fabric tied around his head and was wearing a loose black sleeveless top that showed the toned biceps and made him look younger than his fifty odd years. And, Marius thought, gave him an exotic aura. No wonder the students were all looking up at him, engrossed in whatever he was telling them. 'Student' was an odd word for them really – they were a mixed looking group and some far from young. The table was crammed with empty plates and bowls and glasses and it looked as if things were winding down.

Small groups of people were drinking and eating in the screened dining spaces. On the far side of the room facing on to the garden there were a few sets of rattan sofas and chairs. From one of the sofas Mimi stood up and waved him over. She was holding a book in her hand and she flapped it to get his attention. In front of her on the glass-topped table were a couple of messy piles of the same sort of notebooks and various sorts of folders. Doing some marking no doubt. Marius was reminded of one of his career moves after he left Intelligence, when he thought that perhaps he could be a teacher. It took the students longer than one might expect to realise that giving him their work was the same as throwing it into a black hole. Not that they didn't learn something, but it wasn't what the school had in mind.

He acknowledged Mimi with a slight nod of his head and made his way over. She watched him as he wove between the pillars and tables. Mimi was intrigued and amused by the way he walked. It was almost stately; he looked completely relaxed but very upright, and he walked with a slow, deliberate tread as if each step was being carefully chosen. But the slight swing of the hips from side to side and the glint in his eyes gave a hint that this play at being dignified was really a big joke. She gave him a kiss on each cheek.

— Have a seat. I'm so glad you came. I can put this pile of marking away. I'm ready for a drink. What will you have? She leaned towards him and sniffed the air then laughed. Another brandy?

Marius laughed with her.

— Well done. That's very kind my dear. But I think it's time for one of your excellent Asahi beers. You know the brandy seems to be more of a travelling drink these days.

Mimi sat back down and pulled a blue canvas tote bag from under the table. She held it out and shook it then started packing the folders and books into it. Marius perched on the edge of the sofa opposite and passed them to her. It didn't take long. She hauled the bag onto her shoulder.

— I'll put the orders in. I have to put these things back anyway. Won't be a minute. Large?

— Thank you.

Marius settled back to wait. From where he was sitting he looked straight on to the grounds at the back of Chez Miki. Only the front and sides of the building had been walled in; the rear had been left open, protected by the overhang from the thatch roof. In front of him the darkness was lit by flares placed every so often along the paths that led to the adobe cabins scattered through the gardens. Lights shone through the windows of some of them. Marius' mind wandered to a line from a poem: 'stroked by the light'. Was it Hardy? It had to be; he was the master of creating a whole world in a few words. And who was it that said that?

Marius looked up, away from the lights. A heavy bank of clouds had covered the sky and the darkness was absolute. In darkness – in tenebris. How did that one go? 'Wintertime nighs – twice no one dies'. Marius turned the phrase over in his head: 'Twice no one dies'. Cold comfort. He thought of

Louis, saw him as he'd been last Friday night and felt his throat tighten. Twice no one should die.

— Here you are. Mimi was putting a tall glass of Asahi on the table in front of him.

Marius realised he'd been miles away. A bit disoriented, he pulled himself forward on the lounge and picked up his beer.

— Thanks. Perfect.

— Do itashimashite. You're welcome. You look as if you were doing some serious thinking. Mimi sat opposite him and took a sip of her own beer. It was the same size as the one Marius had and looked huge compared with her.

— Not really. I was trying to remember a poem. Do you ever get a line stuck in your head and even though you know it doesn't matter, you just have to work out where it comes from?

— You know me better than that. You've tried really hard but I still don't get the hang of poetry.

Marius laughed.

— That just shows how distracted I am. How could I forget! What was it you used to say? Stop! My ears are hurting – something like that. And you used to put your hands over your ears and close your eyes.

— How rude. I don't remember saying that. But I do remember that you forced me to learn one poem off by heart in English. English! Why English? French might have made more sense.

— French has its pleasures but I much prefer English poetry.

— You said it would make me sound smart. I can still say some of it. She frowned in concentration and bit her lip. It reminded Marius of the serious little girl who had arrived here twenty years ago. She started reciting:

— Earth has nothing to show. No. Not anything to show – more fair, dull would he be...

— What's this? Literature? Do you never give up?

Neither of them had noticed Takashi. You had to know him quite well to see that he was smiling; his mouth still looked set in the usual straight line but there was just the hint of a lift on one side and his eyes danced. He sat down on the couch next to Marius. With a pseudo-dramatic gesture he took off his head tie and put it on the seat, then he rubbed his hair with the palms of his hands so that it fell back neatly into place. He looked over to where the drumming students were starting to drift off to their cabins.

— They're a nice group but I'm ready for a break. I've asked Yao to bring us some chicken and rice. Does that sound okay?

— Fantastic. Marius hadn't realised how hungry he was.

— Mibou and Lucien should be here soon. You know they're going to play here tonight.

— Speak of the devils.

Lucien was making his way across the room. His large hands rested easily on the handles of the short metal walking sticks and he swung himself along rhythmically, his tiny legs swinging between them. There was a soft clank each time the sticks hit the ground and rattled the metal rings that helped keep his arms attached to the sticks. Mibou followed behind him, looking weighed down with his sax over one shoulder and guitar over the other. Behind him Jojo was trying to see where he was going from behind a bulky black case that he was carrying. Lucien's keyboard. It was as tall as Jojo and awkward to carry. The shoulder strap was useless and the space was too tight to put it on his head or under his arm.

Takashi met them and led them over to the far corner where a wooden platform formed a low stage. Jojo started setting up the instruments and Marius and Mimi made room for Lucien and Mibou on the sofas.

Lucien pulled the sticks off his arms and put them on to

the floor at the end of the couch, glad to be rid of them for a while. He settled back comfortably into the cushions, his tiny feet in the child's sneakers just reaching to the edge of the couch.

— So what's this I hear? You're setting up a Lomé branch of the FBI? He gave one of his lopsided smiles and looked around at them. They all laughed. It was good to have him with them and a relief to laugh a bit at themselves.

— Yes. And Marius is the commissaire. Mimi laughed and gave Marius a mock salute.

Marius smiled, but despite Lucien's sardonic humor he realised it was only half a joke. They did really think of him as being in charge; they had confidence in him. Sure, he had experience that would help but he, more than the others, realised that without professionals – the police and pathologists for example – it was going to be a near impossible task. They still didn't even know exactly how Louis had been killed.

He was saved from his thoughts by Yao, who arrived with a huge wooden platter of steaming chicken. It was simple but good. The chicken golden and crisp, the rice white and fluffy, the pepper sauce fresh and spicy. It didn't take long for them to demolish it.

— What now? Mimi asked, washing her hands in the bowl that Yao had left, and drying them on a small white towel with Chez Miki printed on one end.

Her question wasn't directed to anyone in particular but they all looked at Marius. He looked at Mibou.

— Why don't you go first? Did you get on to Lillian?

— Yes. But I didn't find out very much. You can imagine what it was like. At first she couldn't believe it – and really I'm not surprised. I can hardly believe it myself. Then she said she was talking to Louis on Saturday afternoon. It seems like he was going to have a drink with some friends in the Rue des Bars. You know the one? I don't know the real name – it's the street near the French school where there's a whole lot of bars and food spots. She said it must have been around 5 o'clock in the afternoon. They didn't talk for long because the line dropped out and when she tried to call back she couldn't get through. She was so sad. And it seemed to be worse that she didn't even say a proper goodbye.

Mimi noticed Mibou blinking quickly. He grabbed his beer and took a few gulps.

Marius was starting to feel better. This was more than he'd been hoping for.

— Actually, I think she told you quite a lot. At least we have a time. Now we know where to start from. If we can find out who he was meeting then they should be able to help us work out what happened. Thanks Mibou. I guess she didn't know the exact spot he was going to by any chance?

Mibou frowned and tilted his head to one side, turning his eyes towards the roof as if he was searching up there for a recording of his conversation. After a few seconds he shook his head.

— No. And she seemed a bit surprised that he didn't say which friends he was meeting. But that doesn't mean anything. You know how many friends Louis had.

Mibou leaned across and looked Marius' watch. Then he tapped an imaginary watch on his own wrist and spoke to Takashi.

— Time to start?

Takashi checked the time and nodded.

— Thanks. I put 8.00pm in the new brochure. Did you see what I called you? He looked at Lucien and smiled. Le Grand Duo.

Lucien was already manoeuvering off the couch. He laughed.

— Wait till they see me! He picked up his sticks and headed over to the keyboard.

45

Mibou followed him. He could catch up with the rest of the news from Takashi after they finished playing. The two of them often shared a whisky and did a post mortem on the music after a gig. Takashi S had been a jazz drummer back in his Japan days and he had a finely tuned ear. In fact, he was something of a mentor to both Mibou and Lucien. He was the one who had the idea of getting Mibou and Lucien to play as a duo. Mibou had been reluctant at first. Playing without a drummer or a bass didn't seem like serious music to him. But Takashi had persuaded them to give it a go. Now Mibou noticed that some of the jazz enthusiasts from round town had turned up and he thought that Takashi might have a point.

Lucien set the keyboard to piano mode and he played around with some voicings, glancing over his shoulder with a wry smile as Mibou picked up his sax. Mibou listened to the progression, head on one side, and waited for some more clues. Then he laughed as the chords resolved into 'Oni do do', the popular Nigerian song that they loved to play around with. The smooth notes of the old Selmer didn't really need amplification but he used it anyway.

Takashi smiled. The music pleased him in a way he found difficult to explain; it literally made his heart feel lighter. He felt a bit far away from the others now that there was more space on the couches so he went over and sat next to Mimi. Marius was always struck by the father and daughter resemblance; the same triangular faces with a finely shaped mouth.

Takashi leaned towards Marius and spoke quietly.

— What about Philippe de Brujin? Did you find out anything?

Marius told them briefly about the meeting that he'd set up with Jean-Pierre and Philippe ending with:

— So…he doesn't seem to have an alibi. He was out until late that night. And I suppose that even if he did have an alibi, he could have organised someone else to do it. But when Jean-Pierre talked about Louis, Philippe really seemed surprised. Even shocked. I could be wrong, but I thought he was genuine. Any news on the beachfront Takashi?

Yao came over with a fresh round of drinks. He picked up the last of the dirty dishes and wiped the table. Takashi waited until he'd left then quietly told them how Kodjo Atsou had been shot in the early hours of Saturday morning not far from where Louis' body had been found.

It was the first that Mimi had heard of it. Takashi had been busy with his students when she got back from school. She'd heard of other, unexplained deaths that happened in Lomé, but she couldn't get used to them. Each one was shocking in a different way. And this one much worse because she knew Kodjo's father. Not well, but enough to know that he was just an ordinary fisherman trying to make a living – not even vaguely interested in politics. Sometimes she wondered why she stayed here. Why she didn't move to Japan. But there was something about the people and the place itself that kept her here. And her father of course.

— Now that had to be the military, she said.

Marius agreed.

— Who else would be out at night in that place with that type of gun? Somehow I have a very strong feeling that poor Kodjo's death is connected in some way to Louis'. Same general location, same time. Now I'm even more certain that I have to find out who was meeting with Louis on Saturday night. They might be the last ones to see him alive. It shouldn't be too hard. This is Lomé. People see things and word gets around. I don't have any work for a few weeks so I can find the time.

Marius managed to make a reasonable living from a couple of his past careers. He'd stopped working for Intelligence years ago but the Ghanaian government still paid him to run workshops introducing new recruits to issues and techniques.

Then there were the sessions he ran for trainee teachers at the Winneba Education University. In equal proportion to his complete inability to do simple administrative tasks, he had an impressive way of sharing his own learning with students. He just didn't have whatever it took – and he still didn't know what that might be – to settle into regular work.

Takashi gave his attention back to the music. Mibou had put aside his sax and was using his guitar to give a percussive bass effect and Lucien was improvising around it. They all stopped talking for a while and listened. Spontaneous applause burst out around the room as Lucien finished his solo.

Takashi smiled and clapped. It was just how he'd imagined it would be. His hair had flopped over his face and he pushed it back and nudged Marius to get his attention.

— If I hear anything more about Kodjo I'll let you know. I'm sure Kwame will keep me posted.

Mimi had been leaning over the back of the sofa to watch them playing. She put two fingers on her lips and gave a couple of surprisingly loud whistles then turned back to Marius and Takashi.

— And I'll keep myself au courant too.

7

Marius braced himself for a splash but the moped driver swerved just in time to miss the puddle. He also missed the other mopeds around him and avoided the car on the right that was swerving around the same muddy pool of water that took up half the road. It was morning peak hour and the road was crowded with cars and moto-taxis that swarmed on either side of them, weaving between each other and the cars. It seemed like chaos but most of the time it worked. Marius had only been involved in one minor collision and got a bruised shoulder out of it, though he knew some people who hadn't been so lucky.

The noise of rain blowing against the window and a growl of thunder had woken him some time in the early hours of the morning. But by the time the others had got themselves off to work and school for the day, the storm had blown over and the sun was bright in an unusually cloudless blue sky. The air felt cleansed and fresh. He was inclined to agree with the local wisdom that the harmattan season didn't truly end until there was a storm to clear the air. Now it was officially over.

The storm seemed to have cleared his head as well and he realised that what he had to do was track down those friends of Louis'. Thanks to Lillian at least he had a starting point – the time, the general area. While he was lying awake listening to the rain and thunder he'd come up with the idea of retracing the route that Louis had taken on Saturday night. Start at Louis' compound and end up at the Rue des Bars, put himself in Louis' shoes.

He didn't need a car. In many ways it would be easier to be without one. In Lomé a moto-taxi was never very far away. He'd decided to take one and now he was sitting on the pillion behind the driver, his hands resting on his thighs, enjoying the feel of the bike moving in and out of the traffic.

Coming from Ghana, where mopeds weren't so popular, it had been something to get used to. The first time he'd taken one of the moto-taxis he had no idea what to do, and started to put his hands on the waist of the driver. That felt weird for both of them. The driver shouted at him a few times before he realised he was telling him to hold the chrome bar behind the pillion seat. He'd done that for a while. But then pride kicked in when he saw the locals looking totally relaxed just sitting there with their hands resting on their legs, even mothers with babies tied to their backs. Mopeds weren't the safest mode of transport but on a fine day like today there was something exhilarating about buzzing around town on one. It was cheap too and, he admitted to himself, he loved the adrenaline rush.

After twenty minutes or so the driver pulled into a quiet back street in front of the compound where Louis had lived until a few days ago. It wasn't far from the border with Ghana and Le Jazz Spot was just a few blocks further down towards the town. Marius had been here a few times to pick Louis up in the car. Usually he would park under the shade of the almond trees that spread out onto the street from behind the high plastered wall. The compound was similar to others along the streets around here. From the narrow sandy road all you could see was the wall. The bottom was splattered with dirt from the road and the constant humidity of the tropics had made worn grey patches here and there, but it still retained a lot of the original light umber colour and blended in with the apricot, cream and coral walls along the street.

A heavy wooden gate was set into the wall. Marius opened the gate and stood for a minute surveying the stained white plastered houses that surrounded a compound with a big old mango tree in the centre. The ground was half sand, half soil, and had been neatly swept. In the shade of the tree there were some worn looking plastic chairs. They'd been weathered to a dirty looking grey from their original white. Some discarded beer crates had been upended and looked as if they were used as makeshift tables.

Marius recognised the two women under the mango tree. They lived in the house opposite Louis and seemed to spend most of their time preparing food in this spot. He'd chatted to them before. They were dressed alike in long straight skirts made from yellow and orange patterned African print with a smaller, matching cloth tied around their waists. On the top they wore loose cotton T-shirts. The older woman was sitting on a low wooden stool, a leg on either side of a heavy wooden bowl placed on a small mat, her skirt modestly tucked between her legs. Next to her was a small metal bowl containing water, and a large aluminium pot with a wooden lid was simmering on a brazier. The younger woman was standing on the other side of the bowl, holding a thick wooden stick that still had the contours and markings of a branch. It had been roughly carved to make a smooth, thinner section, which she was using as a handle to pound the mixture in the bowl. After every few down strokes with the stick, the seated woman turned the mixture of plantain and cocoyam.

Marius wandered over to them and peered into the bowl. They must have been there for a while because it was getting close to the desired consistency: elastic dough. They stopped their pounding.

— Fufu? He asked.

— What else? The woman who had been doing the pounding used the cloth tied around her waist to wipe her face and hands. She looked more closely at him then smiled when she realised who it was.

— Mr Marius. Welcome.

— Thank you my friend. Marius had a sudden thought: how much did they know? He tried to phrase the question as cautiously as possible. I'm wondering – perhaps you've heard...

He needn't have worried. The woman helped him out.

— You mean about Louis?

When Marius nodded, she made a loud sucking noise with her teeth and shook her head.

— To think of him being killed like that! And him such a good man.

They were happy to talk about Louis. The almost finished fufu was carefully covered with a damp cloth and the three of them sat on the chairs in the shade of the tree.

Parfait – they used his given name – had been an easy person to have in the compound. Friendly, happy to help out with little things: carrying stuff, even pounding the fufu sometimes. He talked about his family in Benin and often he was over there. But when he was here, the playing! The up and down, up and down, over and over again could get annoying but what can you do? When he played tunes that was different. Yes. He had quite a few visitors but mostly like you, Mr Marius. They'd come and meet up and go out somewhere together. Last Saturday? Of course – they remembered it well. They'd been here under the mango tree, cooking some yam in coconut oil on the brazier. He'd come over to chat with them before going out. Joked with them about how they were always out there cooking. They offered him some but he said he really just liked the smell of the hot oil and that he'd get something in the street. Then left. The time was a bit hard

52

to work out –maybe late afternoon some time? The shade of the mango tree had been over the other side so probably around 4.30.

Marius looked at his watch. He'd been here for over an hour. Not that it was a problem. What was the point in trying to push for quick answers? No, much better to let the conversation take its own course. Anyway, he'd found it therapeutic, listening to the two women talk about Louis.

The women were ready to get back to their fufu pounding. Marius stood up with them and watched as the older woman took the cloth off the wooden bowl, sat back on the little stool and turned the mixture with her hand.

— There's just one more thing you could help with, he said. Have any of his family from Benin been over?

The older woman looked up from where she was sitting.

— Maybe they'll come soon, but no one's been here yet.

— Thank you my friends. Just one more question: do you think I could take a look in his house?

— Of course, just go in. It's not locked.

Marius walked out of the shade into the hot sun and crossed the compound to Louis' house. Behind him the rhythmic thud of the pounding started up again.

He stepped onto a slab of concrete shaded by an extension of the roof and stood in front of the faded blue door. On his left some banana palms grew along the front wall and rustled gently as the air stirred. It felt very strange to be going into the house with Louis no longer here – an invasion of privacy. Marius wasn't even sure what he was looking for, but in a vague way he thought it might give him some ideas.

Inside there were four rooms. Not big but roomy enough. The bare concrete floors looked messy and unfinished, but they were cool under foot and no doubt kept the temperature down. The front door opened directly into a sitting room with glass louvres that opened from floor to ceiling on either side. The louvres were closed and it was stuffy and hot. Marius took a few minutes to open them and the effect was almost immediate; a breeze started to circulate and the heat became bearable.

On his right there was a small kitchen with a window over the sink that looked onto the mango tree and he went in to have a look. A few dishes were soaking in the sink. A couple of crates of empty beer bottles were stacked at the door. Marius wondered who would be coming to clean out his things. One of his brothers from Cotonou probably, but Marius felt pretty sure that the women were right; no one had been in here yet.

He walked back into the sitting room. A television set and a video recorder were sitting on a set of shelves against the wall near the kitchen. There was an old style ghetto blaster on top of the video recorder and the shelves were stacked with boxes of videos and CDs. On the wall opposite, a comfortable looking three-seater lounge looked as it had seen plenty of use. Louis' trumpet was sitting on a stand at the end of the couch. Marius stood for a minute, staring down at it. So Louis didn't have his trumpet with him.

Marius went past the trumpet into the bedroom. Freshly ironed black trousers were laid out on the bed. A silky black shirt on a coathanger was hooked over the door handle. It hadn't occurred to Marius before but looking at the shirt he realised that he'd never seen Louis play his trumpet in anything else. So it seemed very much as if Louis had planned to meet his friends then come back here and get ready for a night jamming around town. That's what he did every Saturday night. But something stopped Louis from doing it last Saturday. That was becoming more and more obvious to Marius, but what was it? Who was it? Why?

There didn't seem to be anything else that seemed odd. Except that Louis was dead and he shouldn't be. All these familiar things, especially the trumpet and the clothes, made the loss too close, too acute, and Marius could feel his insides knotting up. Best to keep moving. He closed the windows and glanced around to make sure everything was as it should be before leaving the house.

The women had placed the cloth back over the fufu in its wooden bowl and were sitting on either side of the pot on the brazier. Goat stew by the smell of it. Marius took his leave and headed out of the compound.

Closing the gate behind him he turned left and walked along the edge of the narrow sandy lane. This is where Louis had walked on Saturday afternoon. Purple bougainvillea spilled over some of the walls and the almond trees threw a bit of shade. Marius liked the quiet streets in this old part of Lomé. Lots of the people in this area had family in Ghana. When the line on the map had been drawn between Togo and Ghana the men in Europe didn't worry that it went right through the lands of the Ewé people. As a result, every day hundreds of men, women and children poured back and forth over the border, and despite the men in uniform it always felt just this side of mayhem. But even though these streets weren't far from the border you didn't get a sense of that here; it was peaceful, not one of the politicised areas of Lomé.

Marius walked for five minutes or so and came to an intersection where the street opened on to a much wider road. If he turned left, he would eventually hit the Boulevard Circulaire that ran from the beach road into Lomé. A few blocks to the right was the border with Ghana. Le Jazz Spot was a couple of blocks down towards the city. It was tempting to call in for a drink and listen to some jazz, but Marius put the idea out of his head. First things first.

Where the lane ran into a wider road, a woman with a baby tied to her back was getting ready to sell some fried fish and okra stew. She picked up a torn piece of cardboard to fan the charcoal in a metal grill and Marius stopped and greeted her.

Yes, she knew Louis. No, he didn't eat there on Saturday.

Maybe up the road? She pointed to a spot under a flame tree up the road towards the border. Marius looked up the sprawling expanse of dirt and sand that served as a road. It was rutted unevenly with channels gouged by heavy rain. Flame trees were planted at irregular intervals along one side of the road. They were in full bloom and Marius could see a few white plastic chairs set out under the bright green and vermillion of one of the trees.

— Thanks Auntie. Namaste. Palms together, he raised his hands to his face, then he turned right and walked up the road towards the chairs.

When he got closer he realised they were set up in front of a little shop. It was a small, square, whitewashed cement building squashed between houses on either side. In large black letters over the doorway was written Qui est libre? Marius smiled to himself. Who is free indeed? It was a saying that was sometimes written on the rattletrap mini-vans that served as buses, but this was the first time he'd seen it used for a shop. It was one of his favourite sayings and as a statement about this small commercial enterprise, it had added piquancy.

Inside the store was dark compared with the bright sun and it took Marius a few seconds to adjust to the light. The shelves were stacked with canned foods, biscuits, local gin and brandy, toiletries. The usual stuff. Marius browsed the small section of spirits and pulled out a brandy bottle. He held it at arm's length and read the label. Cashew brandy. In his opinion the best brandy in the world. It was always worth looking in these little shops. What a find!

The noise of a door slamming made Marius look up and he saw a young man come out of the door at the back of the shop. He was wearing a purple and blue shirt that hung loose over blue jeans. Neatly pressed, he had an alertness and energy in the way he moved and Marius took an instant liking to him and his little shop.

Marius put the bottle amongst the clutter on the tiny counter and the young man slipped behind.

— I like your establishment my son. You have very fine taste in brandy. May I ask what you call yourself?

— Thank you uncle. I'm Duku. He gave a big smile. I do my best. He took hold of the cashew brandy. You'll take this?

— Please. And a bottle of your coldest Star. Tell me Duku, how are all those brothers and sisters of yours?

Duku had been busying himself with money at the till. He paused, still holding a bunch of dirty CFA notes in his hand and stared at Marius. As if he was miming someone being surprised, his mouth dropped open and his brown almond-shaped eyes opened wide. Then he suddenly relaxed and laughed.

— They're well thank you. And you're right. Duku, eleventh born.

Marius smiled and looked pleased with himself. He took the limp bank notes then he picked up his bottle of brandy.

— Thanks. I'll be outside.

Under the dappled shade of the wide canopy of the flame tree he leaned back in his chair. On both sides of him more flame trees lined the road. Vivid clusters of scarlet flowers almost covered the bright, fern-like leaves. He was grateful to the French – or was it the Germans –who had the foresight to plant these trees. Then he thought of Louis. Imagined him sitting here, looking at the same trees.

Duku didn't take long to get the beer. He'd picked it from the bottom of the cooler and Marius noted the frosted coating around the bottle, already starting to vaporise in the humid air.

— Perfect. Why don't you bring yourself a glass and sit down for a minute?

Duku was happy to sit and chat. Once in a while he got up to serve a customer, but business was slow at this time of the day.

An hour or so and a couple of bottles of Star later, Marius had no doubt that Louis had eaten here last Saturday. Yes, Duku knew Marius' tall friend with the round face, the big smile, the trumpet. Duku had a friend who set up a kebab grill outside the shop in the evenings. He remembered last Saturday very well because of some drunk military types who had called in for a kebab. It had been busy and his friend was finding it hard to keep up with the orders. The military types got aggressive and rude and Duku frankly was a bit worried about what they might do. But then Louis had offered to wait for a second cooking so the soldiers could get theirs first. He was grateful to Louis for helping smooth things over and he'd shouted him a beer.

It was clear to Marius that Duku hadn't heard what had happened. He wasn't sure whether to break the news or not. He liked Duku and felt he should tell him. But he also didn't want to be seen asking around about Louis and in Lomé you never knew who to trust, who was listening and taking note. In the end he decided against saying anything. Word would spread soon enough. He thanked Duku and picked up his brandy. He was sorry to leave this little haven with the philosophical name, but the beer had given him a pleasantly upbeat feeling and in a strange sort of way he felt close to Louis as he put together the jigsaw of his last day.

Out from the shade of the flame tree the sun was hot. Marius walked along the side of the road, heading back the other way now, down towards the Boulevard Circulaire. The sprawling street was almost empty. Every so often a business of some sort was set out in the dirt under the shade of a flame tree. Just down from Duku's place a welder was constructing barbecues of different shapes and sizes and Marius recognised the same grill that the woman near Louis' place had been using. He stopped and had a closer look – he could do with one at home. There was one that was a long rectangle and sat on legs so that the grill was at waist height. It looked a bit like a UFO or a robotic alien, and he liked it. He made a quick decision and put a deposit down to have one made. Could be just the thing for Eva's birthday that was coming up in a couple of weeks.

Continuing down the road Marius came to the last of the flame trees and he found himself walking next to a high grey cement wall. Later in the day the wall would throw some shade but right now the sun was overhead and the wall radiated heat and blocked the flow of air. Two hundred metres or so in front of him the street formed a T-junction with the Boulevard Circulaire, a main road linking the beach with the town. He could see the jumble of cars and trucks and bikes almost at a standstill. At least he wasn't sitting in that traffic jam. A block or so before the T-junction a narrow street cut across both sides of the road he was walking down. It was the one on the right he was heading to.

He picked his way around a dip in the road where water had collected after the storm this morning. The sandy surface was soft and porous next to the wall and the marks of car tyres still showed on either end of the puddle. Marius wondered why a car would want to get so close to the wall when the street was so wide and empty. But who knows? Drivers made up their own rules here.

Five minutes later he turned into the Rue des bars. Not its official name but all the locals called it that. Ghanaian Hiplife music was pumping out at an inhuman volume from huge black speakers that were stacked outside most of the places. It felt like a physical onslaught and seemed to intensify the heat. Eating spots and bars lined both sides of the street. They all looked much the same. White plastic tables and chairs were crammed into a covered area that faced the street and was shaded by dried palm leaves, lattice, tiles, corrugated iron or plastic – anything that would give some protection from the sun.

A few people were already eating but it was less crowded than Marius had expected. Of course, this was more an evening area. Why hadn't he thought of that? Anyway, he was here now. At least he could have a good look round. But where to start? He passed a few places, wandering over to each, checking out what people were eating, not sure what he was looking for. Then he stopped and sniffed. Charcoal grilled fish; he was sure of it. Tilapia. At least the noise of the music hadn't affected his sense of smell. He followed his nose to where a wooden sign with a painted fish was hanging from a bamboo pergola. Grape vines twisted around the wooden supports and almost covered the latticed roof. A waist high wall of woven bamboo fenced in the chairs and tables. He realised two things: he always thought better sitting down and he was hungry.

He chose a table in the deep shade against the wall and called the waitress over. Beer and tilapia ordered, he wondered what next. The music up this end of the street wasn't nearly as loud and he found himself tuning in to the lyrics. The music worked on two levels: it had a fast, insistent dance beat with no pretensions on one level, but the mix of languages – he could make out Twi and Ewé at least – making politically savvy comments worked on another level. He liked the way they were having fun with the languages and the music and the ideas and decided it was a big improvement on the old high life, though he couldn't see himself listening to it at home.

The beer came first and he sipped on it and looked at the other customers. At the table alongside him a young couple looked pretty excited to be having lunch together. Behind them a group of men and women wearing matching uniforms seemed to be having some sort of working lunch. No one that Louis would be likely to know. But as he soaked up the atmosphere Marius realised that this was exactly the sort of place that would have appealed to Louis. For a start, he loved grilled tilapia. Then the general ambience of the place seemed right. Maybe it would be worth asking some discreet questions.

The waitress arrived with the tilapia on a big white plate and placed it carefully on the table in front of him. She was slender and pretty, her hair pulled off her face in fine braids, and she seemed friendly and inclined to chat. Marius decided she could be a good starting point.

— This all looks splendid. But before you go, could I ask you a question?

She looked at him a bit suspiciously but nodded, so he continued.

— I wonder if you've seen a friend of mine. I was hoping I might run into him here. He told me this establishment was one of Lomé's best kept secrets and now I can see why.

He smiled at her, hoping his grey hair would make her feel comfortable. It seemed to work because she relaxed a bit.

— Who's this friend?

— Name of Louis, tall chap from Benin. Chubby face, carries round a trumpet in a black case, loves beer and tilapia.

— I think I might know who you mean. He has a very loud laugh.

— That's him.

She shook her head.

— You're not very likely to see him at this time. He's more an evening customer. His friends are here nearly every day – usually around five. You might have better luck then.

Actually, Marius could hardly believe his luck.

— Thank you my dear, you're very kind. I'll come back in the evening some time.

— Good idea. It's a bit more lively then as well.

She picked up the spare cutlery off the table and left him with his fish. He took a minute to admire it before he started to eat. The skin was perfectly charred and succulent looking. Its head and tail poked out from under a pile of sliced red pepper and onion. On one side there was a generous chunk of banku. On the other two little black bowls, one filled with shitoh and the other with a fresh tomato, garlic and ginger puree.

He ate slowly, using the banku to scoop up pieces of fish and sauce. The young couple left and other customers arrived. Two women who looked like sisters came in and sat at the table in front of him. From the number of bags they dumped on the floor it seemed they'd spent the morning shopping. Next to them was a middle-aged couple who, as far as Marius could see, exchanged not a single word during the whole time they were there.

Then, as he was finishing his meal, two men arrived who were harder to place; one with a shaved head and wearing a black T-shirt and jeans, the other maybe ten years older in a short-sleeved business shirt over grey suit pants.

Marius called the waitress over and asked for the bill. As she was putting the empty bowls and cutlery on the tray she leaned towards him.

— Maybe you're in luck, she said softly. She inclined her head towards the two men who had recently arrived. Those two over there might know if your friend's coming. I've seen them together lots of times.

She disappeared into the kitchen again and Marius wondered what to do next. It was obviously his lucky day and he wanted to make the most of it. What would be the best thing? First he had to talk to Louis' friends. But how should he approach it? Pretend that he didn't know about Louis' death? Such deaths were never reported in the media so it would seem normal. Or should he trust them and tell him what he knew? That might let him ask more questions, find out more. Again he found himself wanting to play it safe. Much better to pretend ignorance, he decided. He didn't want to run any risk of attracting the attention of the military police and here it took a long while to know who to trust. Connections through extended families could stretch in all directions like a vast spider web.

When the waitress came up with the bill he took a second or two to bring himself out of his thoughts. He had already put CFA 2000 for the meal under the empty beer glass. He pulled another note out of his back pocket and pressed it into her hand.

— Thank you my dear. You've been most helpful.

She tucked the note into the pocket of her skirt and smiled.

— Thank you uncle. And good luck.

Marius silently concurred. He needed it.

At the table in the front corner near the street the two men – Louis' friends – were drinking beer and waiting for their meal. Marius strolled over to their table.

They stopped talking as he went up to their table and looked up at him. He felt awkward but tried to look casual and hoped that he didn't sound too jovial.

— A thousand apologies for interrupting, but the young lady over there said you might be able to help me. I was hoping to meet a friend of mine. He goes by the name of Louis.

The two men exchanged a glance then the younger man in the black T-shirt looked at Marius as if measuring him for a suit. When he spoke, however, he sounded friendly enough.

— You'd better sit down.

— Thank you. Marius took a chair from the empty table next to them and sat down.

You're a friend of Louis'?

Marius could see the man was still trying to work out whether to trust him or not. The problem of trust was mutual. He decided not to give much away and made up a story that seemed plausible enough.

— I'm a fan of his music. I'm trying to arrange what you might call a little soiree with Louis and a couple of other musicians. My wife's birthday's coming up in a couple of weeks. Manu is the name.

He reached over and exchanged hand greetings with both of them. The younger man gave his name as Dommie and introduced his friend as Ajavon. Dommie was the talker.

Marius was conscious that he stood out as a non-local in this place; it seemed safer to use one of his traditional names – Manu, second born – rather than Marius, the nickname by which he was rather well known in some parts of town.

— It seems that you haven't heard, Dommie said.

— Heard what?

— The news about Louis.

— News? No. Marius did his best to sound surprised.

Dommie lowered his voice and rested his folded arms on the table. Marius could barely make out the words but he knew exactly what to expect.

— It isn't easy for me to tell you this Manu, but the truth is it seems that Louis' fallen victim to some thugs. He's passed away.

— You can't mean he's dead?

— From what we hear it seems pretty certain.

Marius tried to think of a question that would bring the talk around to Saturday night, but without making it obvious.

— How did you find out? he asked.

— Well, I got a bit worried when Louis didn't show up on Saturday night. We were supposed to meet right here for a few drinks to get into the Saturday night mood. I live just up the road there and in the early days when Louis first started coming over here from Benin he used to rent a room next to our house. So we sort of got into the habit of meeting here on a Saturday afternoon. Anyway, it wasn't like Louis not to turn up. He'd always ring or text if he wasn't coming, so I was asking around if anyone had seem him around town on Saturday night. You probably know how he used to go round the jazz bars with that trumpet. It was odd that nobody had seen him at the usual spots but I thought that something must have come up back home and he'd had to leave suddenly. Then I started to hear things about someone found dead on the beach. You can imagine how I felt when I realised that it was Louis. Of course it's still just from word of mouth but it seems pretty certain. Incredible.

Dommie picked up his drink and relaxed back in the chair, clearly relieved to have passed on the news. Marius thanked both of them. He returned his chair from where he'd taken it and walked back along the street.

He had found out what he wanted to know. Louis had never arrived here on Saturday afternoon. And he hadn't gone back to his place. Not with those clothes laid out ready for a night around town.

Marius pieced together what he'd found out about Louis. He had left his place around 4.30 on Saturday afternoon and gone to Duku's shop. There he'd had a beer and a kebab. Lillian rang after he had left the shop, when he was walking down the road to meet his friends at the tilapia place. They hadn't been talking for very long when the line dropped out and Lillian wasn't able to make contact when she tried to ring back. Louis hadn't arrived at the tilapia spot and he hadn't been back to his place to get changed into his clothes that were laid out. So where had he gone? It was a direct route from Qui est libre? to the tilapia place – it had taken Marius about fifteen minutes not counting the stop at the welders to order the barbecue. Down the sprawling sandy road then right into the Rue des bars. But Louis hadn't made that turn. Marius felt as if there was something he should pick up on. What about that broken connection? Heaven knew that lines dropped out all the time here, but what if Louis himself had ended the call? Did he meet someone as he walked down the road? Someone he didn't want Lillian to know about? At least things were getting clearer, but that still left hours and hours between the phone call and when Louis had been killed on the beach. Or at least found dead on the beach. And what about Kodjo's death? What could the connection be between the two deaths? Same night, similar location.

In front of the house opposite him a moto-taxi was dropping off a young woman. Marius waited until she'd paid and then called the driver over. He hopped on the pillion seat and soon they were part of the stream of traffic heading along the Boulevard Circulaire. He relaxed and put his mind into neutral.

8

It was Friday night and Marius was sitting at his usual table in Le Jazz Spot. He wasn't happy. The Bou-Bop band were racing through 'Take Five' and now Krupa had gone off on a long drum solo. Mibou was wandering from table to table, chatting to friends. Marius was thinking about Louis. Since Tuesday he'd made no progress at all. It was as if Louis had disappeared into thin air, then reappeared dead on the beach hours later. On Tuesday Marius had felt as if he was getting somewhere, that luck was on their side. Now he wondered if they would have to give up.

His friend Gabriel, the captain of the border police, had been on leave and it was only yesterday that Marius had been able to get in touch with him. Then it didn't get him anywhere. Marius had hoped Gabriel would have contacts who could give him something extra – feedback on Louis' injuries, for example. But no. A major in the military police, a certain Tete Senyo, had taken control of the case and he was keeping things to himself. All Gabriel had was pretty much the same story that Takashi had overheard. Nothing else.

Marius had other contacts but he couldn't think of any who could pull rank on the major. There was Selina and Eva's cousin Emmanuel, who was a judge of the Supreme Court, but Marius was keeping him in reserve. There would be no point talking to him about it now. What was there to say?

Marius felt with every bone in his body that Louis' body had been planted on the beach to cover up something else, but he didn't even have a plausible theory, let alone any evidence. No. He could only contact Emmanuel either as a last resort, or when they did have a theory and evidence. He was beginning to think they might never be in that position.

Marius watched Mibou stroll back to the join the band. He casually took his sax off the stand and attached it to his lanyard then came in with the others on the exact beat for the final head. How did he do that? There was an uncertain round of applause as Krupa finished his drum solo and Mibou led them back into the melody. Marius didn't join in and sipped absent-mindedly on his beer, staring into the distance, lost in thought.

He heard a soft murmur of konban wa in his ear and he looked up to see Mimi laughing at him.

— Mimi my dear. I'm very happy to see you.

He pushed his chair out and stood up. She gave him a hug and a kiss on both cheeks, waved to Akosua and mimed the idea of a bottle and some glasses, then sat down and looked at Marius. In profile, his long brow and the gravitas of his mouth with its protruding lower lip could almost have been the Roman general from whom he got his nickname.

— You were looking pretty serious when I came in.

— I was thinking about Louis.

— We've been wondering what you've found out.

— Not as much as I'd like.

He told her about Tuesday and how Louis hadn't made it to the meeting with Dommie and Ajavon. And how the leads he'd tried had gone nowhere.

The band finished another piece and they joined in the applause. Marius poured himself a glass of beer and topped up Mimi's wine.

Mimi thought about what he'd just said. Louis seemed to

disappear some time around 5.00 on Saturday afternoon. She waited until the music started up again then pulled her chair a bit closer to Marius and spoke softly.

— Now that we know that Louis never made it to that meeting, it makes me think that something I heard today might be connected. It could be nothing, but I'll tell you anyway. You always say that everything's grist to your mill!

— And so it is. I'm intrigued.

— Well…I was having lunch with some friends at school today and they told me about a horrible thing that happened on Saturday afternoon. Last Saturday. They didn't go into much detail, but apparently they were taking part in an opposition rally and someone shot into the crowd. Sounds pretty bad.

— Interesting. Typical that it didn't get reported. Are you sure that's all they said? Did they say what route the rally took? Where they were? Right now I can't think of any possible connection but you just never know. Anyway, thanks for telling me.

— I'm not sure. I didn't ask. It was lunchtime and we had to get back to class. But they'll be here later. You can ask them yourself.

— Why not? But I don't want them knowing about Louis and what we're trying to find out. You didn't say anything to them did you?

— I almost did! But I changed what I was saying just in time. I don't think they noticed.

— So, now we have three – let's call them events. Marius counted off three fingers on his left hand as he went through them. One: Saturday afternoon sometime just after 5.00, Louis seems to vanish into thin air. Then around 2.00 am he reappears dead on the beach just down from the little boat harbour. Two: Kodjo is shot not far away from the boat harbor, also in the early hours of Sunday morning. Three: On that same Saturday afternoon there's a protest rally and shots are fired into the crowd. We have two different times and two possible connections. There's the afternoon and the mystery of Louis not turning up at the Rue des bars and now the rally. Then there's the early morning and two bodies: Louis and Kodjo. One taken to with a machete, the other shot. I can't see how they're connected but somehow I can't see how they're not. That doesn't make much sense does it? What do you think Mimi?

— I don't know what to think. Mimi stared into her glass of wine as if the answers might be in there, then she continued. Things happen all the time here. You know, people get handed out some really bad treatment and we all sort of carry on as if it isn't happening. I wonder if it's just that now we're thinking about Louis things seem more connected than they really are.

Mimi felt she wasn't being much help but it was too confusing. Not only that, but she was also nervous about singing tonight. It wasn't rational – of course she could do it. But the nerves were eating at her anyway. She took a sip of wine and leaned back to watch the band. Out of the corner of her eye she saw that some people had just come through the gate. They stood there uncertainly for a minute or two as if they were new to the place. Then Mimi recognised them.

She turned back to Marius and pointed to the entrance.

— Hey. There they are.

Mimi stood up and waved Jenny and Sarah over. Marius stood up as well and rearranged the chairs around the table. He watched them stop to chat to some people at one of the tables and whispered to Mimi:

— I'll make up some sort of story about why I'm interested in the rally, so don't be surprised by what you hear.

Mimi was relieved to see them. When they'd said they'd come tonight to listen to her sing she hadn't been certain they were serious.

Introductions were made and they all sat down. Mimi poured some wine for Jenny and Sarah.

Marius felt a sharp punch on his arm and looked up at Mibou who was standing behind him and waving around a tumbler full of whisky as if it was some sort of trophy he'd won.

— Hey, hey, hey. His voice went up and down in a sing-song sort of way. Yebba! Lighten up.

Mibou pulled a chair from the table next to them and sat down. Marius watched him clink glasses with Jenny and Sarah. Amazing how he could generate an upbeat mood without really saying anything. For sure it was what Marius needed right now.

Mibou looked hard at Mimi, mock-serious, and raised his glass.

— To mon élève. He laughed. It always seemed to him a big joke that Mimi, the real teacher, could be a student of his. The idea of being a teacher – and he was, in fact, a good one – didn't fit with his image of himself as a jazz man in the Charlie Parker tradition.

He leaned over closer to Sarah and Jenny and lowered his voice in a pretend whisper:

— You know Mimi, she's not big n'est? But wait until she sings! Watch out Dee Dee!! Then he leaned back and looked at them sternly. I hope you're staying?

They assured him that it was to listen to Mimi that they'd come here tonight. Mimi felt a bit embarrassed but she was used to Mibou. If you went along with him things usually worked out somehow.

Mibou allowed himself to be serious for a minute. He, more than anyone, knew how nervous Mimi was, even though she was hiding it. If this were a big concert, he'd be feeling the same.

— Let's bring you in straight after the break with two to

start with and then again at the end. How about an upbeat La vie en rose to start with?

Mimi felt happy with that and she nodded.

— Then what?

— A surprise?

Her stomach churned at the thought – she hoped Mibou was teasing. She shook her head.

— Let's make it Summertime, she suggested, trying not show her panic. And at the end?

— Maybe two more. We'll see how it goes.

— What if they don't like me?

— They'll like you. Trust me. Then he laughed and refilled her wine glass from a bottle of wine on the tray of drinks Akosua had just brought over. You'll need some more of that before you start. He shook his finger at her in what he imagined was a schoolteacher sort of way and wandered off to chat to some friends at the next table.

Mimi drank the wine slowly. She felt better. Nervous but excited. She let the others talk around her and thought of her mother; it gave her confidence, knowing she shared some musical genes. The image that came into her mind was of Miki wearing a long strapless red dress with a flowing red scarf and singing into a microphone. That was how she looked in the photo on the television set in the living room. Mimi poured herself another glass of wine, topped up the other glasses and smiled to herself as she listened to Marius talking to Jenny and Sarah.

He was explaining to them how he was thinking of writing a piece about the rally on Saturday for the Ghana Review. They told him much the same story as Mimi had, but Jenny could give him an approximate time when they heard the shots and it must have been close enough to 5 o'clock – the time when Louis was talking on his mobile to Lillian. They were a bit vague about where they were – maybe not too far from the

Presidential palace. Then Sarah had an idea. She thought she could arrange for her friend Jacques to talk to Marius. He'd probably be happy to share what he had seen if it meant that the shooting got some press coverage. Marius warmed to the role of journalist. Perhaps he would write something after all, and send it to over to his friends on the Review. At least it would keep his conscience clear and really it was about time he made some sort of stand. He didn't particularly like how cynical and world-weary he'd become. There was no need to put his name to the article, so it would be a way of protesting without ending up on a strike list.

Sarah and Marius were exchanging phone numbers when Mibou finally made it back to the stage and introduced Mimi. Marius watched as she walked up to the microphone. She looked tiny compared with Mibou, even in her high-heeled purple sandals. Not a sign of nerves. Marius surprised himself by feeling a bit like a relieved like a father. He hoped Takashi would be able to make it here one of these days. Marius had heard Mimi sing twice now and each time her voice had taken him by surprise. Mibou was right. It was a big voice and brought to mind big names. Not just her voice but the beat, the phrasing. It sent a tingle up the spine.

Mimi didn't really hear the loud clapping as she came back to the table She felt disoriented but happy and realised that her hands were shaking. Sarah leaned over and filled up her glass again.

— Fabulous! She whispered.

Marius touched her glass with his.

— Well done my dear. I can see your name in lights. First Ouagadougou. Then Montreux.

Mimi just smiled and settled back to enjoy the music. The last song of the night was St Louis' Blues and she ended up singing an impromptu duet with Mibou. It seemed exactly the right thing to do and she realised that this evening was like a memorial to Louis. That's probably why it was so crowded and when she thought about it, that's how things tended to happen here. Word just got around.

9

Takashi stopped swimming when he drew level with the Beach Bar. He closed his eyes and stretched out his arms. The salty water took the full weight of his head and he moved his feet gently up and down to keep himself afloat. The water under him rose and fell as unbroken waves rolled towards the shore. He felt completely relaxed and happy, suspended in dark weightlessness with the sun warm on his body and the tepid water rocking him gently. When he sensed from the movement of the water that he was getting close to the shore he reluctantly opened his eyes and felt with his feet for the sandy bottom. He let a wave break and walked through the foam behind it to the shore. For a minute or two he stood in the clear water at the very edge of the tide line and looked up the beach towards the village of Agkamé. The two figures coming towards him were still a fair way off but he could recognise Kwame by the sauntering walk. Next to him was a girl or maybe an older woman. Kwame he was expecting. The text had just said '8 tmrow yr place'.

By the time Takashi had dried himself and pulled a T-shirt over his wet swimming shorts the two had arrived. Kwame took off his dark glasses and greeted Takashi with the usual handshake.

— Hey Takashi. How's it going eh? He put a protective hand on a shoulder of the young woman standing quietly next to him and explained: This is Ama. She was a very good friend of Kodjo. There's something she saw that night – could be interesting.

Takashi guessed Ama was in her early twenties. Coming along the beach, she looked short compared with Kwame but now he could see that she was quite tall. Her hair had been straightened and pushed back from her face with a black band giving emphasis to her wide cheekbones. A sleeveless blue flowered top over a denim skirt gave her a fresh sort of look but she seemed shy and unhappy and looked down at the ground as Takashi and Kwame exchanged their greetings.

Now she tried to smile at Takashi but he thought it made her look even sadder.

— I didn't want to say anything in the text I sent, Kwame explained. Ama's too frightened to talk in the village about what she saw, but she trusts you.

Kwame noticed Takashi's raised eyebrow and laughed.

— You're not exactly the biggest gossip around!

Takashi smiled at Ama.

— Welcome. Let's find somewhere to sit.

He led them over to the Beach Bar. Opening time was still a couple of hours off, but white slatted chairs and tables were permanently left out under an open-sided palm-thatched extension to the elegant timber and glass bar. It was still early and Takashi arranged some chairs in the morning sun that filtered through the lattice at the eastern end of the annex. Ama sat between Kwame and Takashi. She perched on the edge of her chair looking ill at ease.

Takashi felt for her. His chin resting on his cupped hands, he leaned forward and spoke quietly to her.

— You must be feeling very sad.

Ama looked at him and nodded. Her eyes with their curly dark lashes were big with tears that spilled over and started to roll slowly down her face. Every so often she used a finger to wipe them away in an unconscious gesture.

Takashi knew that there was nothing he could say that would help. When he was struggling with his grief after Miki had been shot, the well-meaning people who tried to comfort him with platitudes just made things worse and nearly drove him crazy.

Kwame had been sitting back, gazing at the boats fishing on the other side of the reef. His sunglasses were almost the same colour as his face and it gave him a half sinister, half comical look. Now he pushed them up onto his head and moved his chair a bit closer.

— Ama and Kodjo wanted to get married, he explained, but Ama's family have other ideas.

Ama looked up and half-smiled at Kwame. She sounded matter of fact but Takashi could hear the bitterness.

— Yes. There's some old man in Kpalime they think I should marry. But Kodjo's father was helping us. He thought he could persuade my father eventually. Kwame knows all about it.

She looked exhausted and desolate. The silent tears continued running down her face.

Kwame pulled out a fairly clean handkerchief from the back pocket of his shorts and handed it to Ama.

— It was Kodjo's father who told me about what Ama saw, he said to Takashi. Then he turned to Ama. Do you want me to tell him?

Ama shook her head.

— No. I'm okay really. She pushed away some more tears impatiently with the handkerchief and left heavy blurred marks across the tops of her cheekbones. Kodjo and I had a place where we used to meet. We'd wait until our families were asleep – usually at two or three in the morning – and then go to a place behind the Ritz. You know where there's a sort of courtyard at the back?

Takashi nodded. A good choice he thought.

— Well Kodjo needed to have a pee so I stayed there while he went out to those trees just by the road that goes to the Marina restaurant. He hadn't been gone very long at all. I was just sitting with my back against the wall and feeling a bit sleepy when I heard loud bangs. I didn't realise it was shots at first – just this really loud noise – and I rushed out from behind the Ritz to see what was going on. I couldn't see Kodjo anywhere but I heard a car, then I saw the back of it as it went along the road. It was quite close. It didn't have any headlights on but the red lights at the back lit up as it went round the corner. Then it went away really fast towards the highway. I was sure something awful had happened. At first I couldn't see Kodjo anywhere, then I looked down. And Kodjo was just lying there.

Ama stopped to get control of herself but her voice was choked. She shook her head then wiped her eyes with her hands as if trying to get rid of the image.

Takashi waited until Ama had settled back in her chair and had control of herself.

— Ama, did you happen to notice anything else about the car? Any letters or numbers? Take your time – try to bring the picture of the car into your mind.

She nodded. For a minute or two she sat very still and looked out over the sparkling water, frowning in concentration. Takashi watched some busy white crabs pushing tiny balls out of holes in the wet sand and waited.

She turned back to him, her eyes still screwed up with the effort of remembering.

— I'm sorry. I still can't remember much. Just that the car was grey. A light coloured grey, almost silver. And it looked quite new and sort of big.

Not much to go on there, Takashi thought, but he didn't let her see that he was disappointed.

— Nothing else?

Ama shook her head. She felt as if she'd failed a test.

Takashi looked at her worried face. The frown had gone, but her eyes looked frightened and she had withdrawn into herself again. He didn't want to make things any worse for her than they were already so he gave her an encouraging smile.

— Don't worry, maybe something will come to you later. And you've already told me so much. Come on. Let's have something to eat. I don't know about you two but I'm getting hungry. How about some fish and banku?

Kwame took no persuading at all but Ama was shaking her head and making excuses.

Takashi realised she probably felt uncomfortable about eating in a strange place that was outside her own experience. But good food always made things better.

— Come on, he persisted. It's been cooked for the guests anyway and there's always too much. We'll just sit outside in the garden.

Ama gave in and Takashi led them through the back entrance and into the gardens of Chez Miki. He installed them at a table in one of the little tree-shaded rotundas that were dotted around the grounds.

The food organised and more comfortable in some dry clothes, he joined them with a tray of drinks. Beer for Kwame and himself, cola for Ama. She'd gone inside looking for the toilet and Takashi was happy to have a few minutes to talk to Kwame by himself. He'd been thinking about the car and where it came from and realised he didn't know much about how the shooting was done. Or even if anyone knew that the shots came from the car.

—How certain is it that there's a connection between the car and Kodjo's death?

— We're sure. There're two things, yeah? One is that Ama seems to have been on the scene pretty quick and she didn't see, or for that matter hear, anyone else. You know, like soldiers out on a drunken spree – usually what you'd think it would be. They'd have to use juju to disappear that quick. Then there's the thing I didn't want to talk about when Ama was here. Kodjo's body was sprayed with bullets. I didn't see his body myself, but Kweku told me he saw at least six bullet holes. It looked as if whoever did it just kept firing rounds. Like a drive by, yeah?

—Was he hit from behind or in front?

— From the front and across the chest sort of area. We figure that he'd just zipped up and was standing there in the trees next to the road – probably gazing around as you do. He would have seen them driving past. How they came to see him we don't know. It was nearly a full moon that night but even so he must have been very unlucky.

Ama had come up quietly while they were talking and slipped into her chair. She gave a sort of a laugh.

— Unlucky! You should have seen what he was wearing. His lime green T-shirt with the pink sparkly writing on it. I was teasing him about it – you know we were meeting in secret and here he was with this T-shirt. She smiled as she remembered, though her eyes looked huge through the unshed tears. He loved that T-shirt. His cousin brought it back from the US for him.

— What did it say?

Kwame laughed.

— I know that T-shirt. It said something about jumping at the Ritz.

— Putting on the Ritz! Ama corrected him.

Even she couldn't help laughing. It felt good to talk about Kodjo as if he was still alive. Then she remembered the thing that she'd thought of while she'd been walking back from the toilet. She felt a bit shy and her voice was hesitant and soft.

— I think I might have remembered something else small, small about the car.

Takashi only half heard her.

— The car? he asked.

— It's probably nothing.

Kwame was looking a bit impatient, but Takashi was worried she might decide not to tell him. One of her hands was resting on the table and he covered it with his own and spoke to her very gently.

— Take your time. Anything you can tell me is more than I know.

He took his hand away and waited.

— Well, I think I might have seen something on the bumper thing at the back of the car. It was black and had some sort shiny stuff on it. It looked like the letters 'G' and 'i'. Capital G and small i. Then maybe an L but I'm not so sure. She surprised herself by remembering so much and sat back relieved, sipping her cola through a straw.

Takashi raised an eyebrow at Kwame.

— Any thoughts?

— Sounds like it could be a bumper sticker, yeah?

Takashi nodded. He felt at a loss. Bumper stickers weren't really his thing. They weren't visible like the pithy sayings that were written on all the transport vehicles. Those you couldn't miss. There was something though. A sticker would surely be chosen to make a personal statement – like a football team logo, or 'my other car's a Mercedes'. That was a popular one here.

— It might rule out anyone official, like the military and the gendarmes.

— Unless they have their own stickers. Maybe it says 'guns for sale'. Kwame made a wry face.

Takashi saw Yao arriving with the fish. Good. They clearly weren't going to get any further and he was really hungry now. He took the bowl of warm soapy water and a clean cloth and passed it to Ama.

— Thanks so much for coming over, he said. It was a brave thing to do and I'm grateful.

Ama just smiled and washed her hands. She scooped up a piece of fish, then some banku and some pepper sauce and looked around her at the little rotundas with their neat hedges and shady tees, the smooth terracotta curves of the drumming centre and beyond that the soaring palm thatch of the restaurant. She'd never been in such a beautiful place.

Delicious, she said. Thank you.

10

At 3am on Saturday night Silvers, the spot to go to, was still packed with a youngish crowd of Africans and Europeans making the most of the balmy night. They were jammed around tables and chairs in a paved garden and a 6-piece band was playing a mix of reggae and seventies and eighties pop covers.

Mibou was dancing with an English woman with spiky red hair. He hoped that if he didn't move his feet too much and just waved his arms around he'd get through the ordeal without anyone noticing how drunk he was. The woman was singing along to the music and making energetic pointing gestures that he found disconcerting but interesting at the same time. He couldn't dance to save himself but there she was completely in time without even thinking about it. In more sober moments, he enjoyed the irony that he, the black man, was the one who had no natural rhythm at all. Every so often she made a pointing gesture at him and caught his eye and he tried to oblige by pointing at the stars and letting out a cry of 'yebba', but it seriously threw him off balance so he stopped. At last the piece finished and she yelled something in his ear that he didn't catch, gave him a kiss on the cheek, and disappeared into the crowd.

Half an hour earlier Mibou had been up on the stage belting out 'Hotel California'. He and his friend Alex, a guitarist from Cotonou, had commandeered the guitars from the band and drunkenly taken over, battling it out in homage to Felder and Walsh until the drummer got fed up and stopped playing. It was as Mibou was getting down off the stage that the English woman had pulled him on to the crowded dancing area in front of the band. All of that had sobered him up a bit and he felt reasonably in control of himself as he wandered back to the table he was sharing with some musicians.

There was an informal hierarchy in the group, loosely based on musical talent. Mibou was at the top with Alex a close second. Then Victor, the young Ghanaian jazz pianist and a couple of middling to fair trumpeters – Mibou always called them les Lionels, because they shared that name and always seemed to hang out together. And then almost at the bottom there was the short self-important bass player who strutted around like a puffed up toad. Mibou couldn't be bothered to remember his name and thought of him only as 'the bad bassist'. It wasn't just that he couldn't play; he had no idea how bad he was. He'd managed to get the ear of the President or someone close to him and Mibou didn't trust him and didn't like him. Anyone who was prepared to orchestrate the trite concerts and cultural events that the President demanded in the name of authenticity had to be minable in Mibou's books. And much as he tried, he couldn't quite get rid of a feeling of resentment towards the amount of money this idiot was paid for perpetuating bad music. Not that Mibou wanted to do it. He'd been asked once and had turned it down. Right at the bottom of the hierarchy was the silent, stoned young man he knew only as the Rasta, a djembe player who tagged along like a stray dog looking for a home. Mibou watched him sliding his hands on and off the drum between his knees, eyes closed, head thrown back, and wondered how many lice were crawling around in the long straggly dreadlocks.

It was the time of night when drinks just kept appearing

on the table. Someone had put a beer glass filled with whisky in front of Mibou. He waved it around in thanks and drank it down in one go. Then he pretended to breathe out the fumes like a dragon, laughed as if it was the funniest joke in the world, poured beer into the same glass and drank it straight down as well.

Someone suggested food and they all squeezed into an old taxi held together almost entirely by rope and wire. One of the back doors wouldn't open and the other one wouldn't close but it finally started and fifteen minutes later set them down safely in a dark side street in front of a shabby low-roofed building. A few rickety looking tables and chairs were crammed under a corrugated iron roof that jutted out from the front wall. On the wall the word 'Sunrise' was painted in black. Seeing the sun come up from here was a ritual for local musicians looking for a meal after they finished their gigs and collected their money.

Mibou had nodded off during the taxi ride and his head felt heavy and dull. He remembered some cola nut that he had in his pocket and chewed on that. Better. Whisky. Guinness – Nigerian of course, much better than the feeble Irish variety. Much better. By the time the food arrived – steaming piles of spaghetti with chili and tomato sauce – the tiny part of Mibou's brain that had been keeping track of how drunk he was succumbed and he achieved full intoxication. Success.

On his left Alex was deep in an argument with les Lionels about the relative merits of Thierry Henry and David Beckham. On his right the bad bassist – apparently he went by the name of AJ – was making sucking noises as he shovelled spaghetti into his mouth. The Rasta was still tapping on his djembe, ignoring the plate of spaghetti. Victor – younger and wiser – had gone home.

Mibou's euphoria had peaked five minutes ago and his mood was sliding quickly into maudlin depression. He turned his back on Alex and leaned his elbows on the table, peering sideways in mock horror at the sight of AJ drinking coke. Then he reached out, meaning to point to the bottle. His finger seemed to have a will of its own and connected with the bottle, not what he had intended. The bottle rocked, tipped and started to spill onto the plate of spaghetti. AJ grabbed it and moved it out of reach.

— You'll never get drunk drinking that poison, Mibou slurred. Hey. D'y know 'bout Louis?

AJ scraped the last of the chili sauce off his plate and sucked it off his fork. He put the plate to one side and pushed his chair a little further from Mibou.

— Yeah. I heard.

Mibou turned heavily back to Alex and grabbed his shoulder.

— Y' hear 'bout Louis?

Alex stopped talking mid-sentence and suddenly the whole table was silent and looking at Mibou. Even the group at the table next to them seemed to feel the different texture of the air and lowered their voices.

Mibou struggled hard to stop himself, but tears started running down his face anyway. He reached for his glass of whisky, missed, tried again then raised it for a toast.

— Here'sh to Louis. He'sh good man Louis. There'sh no one c'd play trumpet like Louis.

Even the Rasta stopped drumming and raised a glass and they all drank to Louis.

— You know if Louis was here, Alex said, trying lighten the mood, he'd call you a baby for crying.

Mibou threw his head back and laughed.

— Y're right. 'S what he'd say.

The awkward moment passed. Stories were shared about Louis' playing. Alex knew the Brassafrique band that Louis played with and talked about a contract the band was about to sign. Louis might finally have got some recognition outside West Africa. That made Mibou sad again.

— 'Stead he's dead on a beach.

— You mean he was found dead on the beach? One of les Lionels asked.

Mibou thought he was lowering his voice but his exaggerated whisper could easily be heard all over the room. He still couldn't seem to get his tongue to work properly and his mouth wouldn't make the sounds he was hearing in his head.

—Sh'what they say. Louis doin' drugs and bam! Louis! He moved his head slowly and dramatically from side to side. Then he leaned forward and the others did the same. Don't tell anyone – no one at all – but 's not true. We know f'sure 's not true. But remember – he put a finger on his lips – 's top secret. Not a word. Shhhhh.

A few other musicians from Silvers turned up. Tables were pushed together and drinks ordered. They joked around with Mibou and Alex about their guitar duel and argued about which of them had 'won'; it had already become local music legend. What could they call it? Not a rumble in the jungle. Alex came up with guerre des guitars, and so it became.

The sun was up when they somehow managed to settle the bill and leave. AJ had driven his car there and he took charge of Mibou, who had got to staggering drunk stage. Mibou found it amusing to repeatedly tell AJ he'd sold his soul to the devil. AJ thought Mibou was a fool to squander his musical talents on playing jazz instead of milking it for money, but he kept that to himself. He quizzed Mibou some more about Louis but Mibou had reclined the seat as far back as it would go and was out to it.

It was the stifling heat in the room and the sun coming straight onto his bed that woke Mibou at midday on Sunday. His mouth tasted of iron filings. He remembered playing with Alex and dancing with some English woman then eating spaghetti at Sunrise but the rest was a blank. He couldn't remember how he got home. Idiot, he thought to himself. He hoped he hadn't done anything really stupid and he pulled the pile of clothes on the floor over to the bed. They felt limp and greasy and reeked of smoke. He went through the pockets. His wallet was still there but there was no money left in it. Surprisingly his mobile was still in the back pocket of his jeans. He checked it. There was a message from the English woman whose name turned out to be Pamela. 'c u at Maxime's at 7' it said. He felt relieved. Things could be worse.

11

At the same time that AJ was dropping Mibou off at his house on Sunday morning, Marius and Takashi had been jogging for at least ten minutes. The stiffness in Marius' legs and knees had almost gone and he was starting to feel as if he might even enjoy the run. He looked at Takashi running alongside him and wondered if it was his new super-light running shoes that made it seem so easy for him. He thought not; more likely all the exercise he did. Perhaps he should start swimming in the mornings as well. He tried to imagine it but when he thought about the drive and the organisation involved his mind recoiled. Anyway, he was feeling pretty good now and his old plimsolls were nicely worn in to the shape of his feet.

He looked around at the other runners. There must have been almost a hundred who had started out with them. Some self-appointed organisers were at the head of the group. One of them ran with a whistle permanently clamped between his teeth and blew a loud two beat rhythm. The others kept a chant going and some of the joggers around Marius and Takashi were joining in. The leaders were taking them criss-crossing through Lomé's streets.

Marius thought about the first time he'd gone on this run. It had been in 1990, just after he'd moved to Togo. His work in the Soviet Union had ended with glasnost and there was a general feeling of optimism about change towards democracy. He'd been happy to work on a doctorate at Togo University and even Selina didn't know – at least at the time – that he was working undercover for the Rawlings government.

He was friends with some of the students who had been on trial for handing out anti-government pamphlets. Of course the RPT had come down hard on the riots that followed and there were curfews and laws against meeting in groups of more than five. Word got around about a Sunday morning jog and it became the only safe way to meet. The chants they sang as they jogged were witty and anti-government. It was a sort of safety valve and gave them a feeling of solidarity as well as a chance to talk politics.

They always met at the same spot on the beach – in front of the volleyball nets – then ran through the Lomé streets, picking up runners as they went. Some would start at the beach then drop out of the run when the group reached their house. Others would wait until the bunch of runners got somewhere near their house and would join in for a while. Over the years there had been times when the government took the pressure off and things seemed almost normal. But any direct opposition brought out the riot police and the military. Marius found it hard to see a time when real change would happen.

These days he and Takashi met up to enjoy the exercise and a chat. They usually left the other runners when they passed a favourite drinking spot of theirs on the west lagoon, not far from the house where Takashi and Mimi had lived for their first few years in Lomé. Today the run was a safe way to thrash out their ideas about Louis. It would be so much easier if only they felt safe using their mobiles. But they didn't.

Marius could feel the sweat starting to bead on his forehead and he wiped it with the sleeve of his T-shirt. Perhaps he should ask Takashi to get him some of those sweat bands, though he couldn't quite see himself wearing them. Why not he wondered? What statement was he trying to make in his old shorts and T-shirt?

At least the roads were mostly flat and the jogging pace was only a bit faster than a walk. He could chat with Takashi and keep up with the other runners around them without getting too out of breath. They had to move from the road onto the footpath to let some cars through and Takashi went ahead. He waited until Marius caught up with him again and then continued where they'd left off.

— Kwame came to see me again yesterday. He brought along a young woman called Ama. It seems that she was Kodjo's girlfriend. She was so sad. Anyway, she told us some more about the night Kodjo was shot.

He told Marius what Ama had told him. How she'd seen the car driving away.

— Did you say it was a silver colour? Marius asked.

— That's what she thinks. It was dark of course, but not pitch black because the moon was almost full that night. She said light grey, almost silver and she had the impression it was quite new. And big, whatever that means. She thinks she saw something on the back bumper bar – maybe the letters G and i. Capital G, small i. In black with some shiny stuff on them is how she described them. If only it had been the number plate; then I'd feel as if we had something to go on.

— They probably took the number plate off. Otherwise you'd think she would have seen that too. Sounds like she's pretty observant, considering.

— Of course. Why didn't I think of that?

— Seems as if Ama was lucky not to be shot as well. I wonder how they didn't come to see her.

— They'd made a hell of a noise with the shooting. I guess they knew they'd wake up the village and just wanted to get out of there. And the way the road comes close to that stand of palms and then makes almost a right-angle turn means that they were driving towards Kodjo, but away from Ama. She said the headlights were off.

— Interesting. It mightn't mean anything but that's the colour of Philippe de Brujin's car. You know we haven't completely ruled him out yet. My intuition tells me he had nothing to do with it, but that could easily be wrong.

Takashi looked sideways at Marius and laughed.

—Not since I've known you! Anyway, I have a theory about the car.

— Which is?

— I think whoever was in the car didn't want anyone to know they'd been along that road. I was thinking it might be that they thought Kodjo had recognised them. I'm saying 'them' because if the shots came from the car, it's probably not going to be from the driver. If I'm right, it could be because it was someone easy to recognise. Or it could be the type of person who would stand out to Kodjo.

— Like a European. Or someone in uniform: gendarme, military, that type of thing.

Takashi wiped his forehead with the blue and green sweatband on his wrist. It matched his Sugoi running top.

— Yes. It could be that.

Marius tried to visualise the road that went through Agkamé. He saw a loose sandy track that wandered between a maze of shanties – a mess of black plastic, woven palm leaves, container crates, anything that could be used to make a shelter. He'd driven along it many times to get to the Marina, a fairly upmarket seafood restaurant run by a French expat. The parking area there was as far as he'd gone.

— Where exactly does that road go to? I've only been as far as the Marina.

— It looks as if it finishes at the restaurant. But if you go around the back of the parking area to the left, there's a gap in the fence a bit further along and the road becomes more basic, just a couple of tyre tracks with long grass growing in the middle. It finishes just to the right of the little boat harbour the Agkamé fishermen use to moor their boats – the ones that go deep sea fishing. From what I heard those soldiers saying, that's roughly where they found Louis' body.

— So what are you thinking?

— I'm thinking that maybe Louis was taken to the beach in that car.

— Why?

— I don't really know, but it's such a coincidence. The timing's the main thing. Think of the village. Once the Marina is closed, no one goes along that road. Why would they? It's not as if the fishermen have cars! Whoever was out there must have had a special reason for being there in the first place and for not wanting to be seen. Maybe they just panicked and shot Kodjo. But of course it's also possible that they did it to intimidate the village. There could have been a rumour about an opposition supporter that set it off. I haven't ruled it out. Who knows what the RPT militias get up to? Then there's the possibility that they were doing an arms deal or a drug deal for that matter. I have a hunch that the reason they were there is because they killed Louis. I don't know how or when. But that's what I think. If we could find out whose car it is we would find the killer – or killers more likely.

— Whoever killed Louis had access to the cocaine that was planted on Louis, so they could easily have been dealing drugs. But how the hell did Louis get caught up in it? I'm coming around to thinking that he was probably dead before he was taken to the beach. One way or the other, he'd have to have been taken there against his will.

— The machete might have been used after he was dead, just to make it look as if it was the work of the Beach Boys.

— In a way I hope so. A machete! It makes me sick just thinking about it.

Marius stopped talking as the runners around him bunched together on the side of the road to let some more cars through.

He looked at his watch; they'd been running for a bit over half and hour. Still about twenty minutes or so before they would get to the lagoon. The runners spread back on to the road and Marius felt free to talk again.

— I've been trying to think of who I could get to help us but I'm not getting anywhere. You know my friend Gabriel, the captain of the border police? Well I finally managed to contact him yesterday; he'd been on leave it seems. You know I was hoping he might have more info about Louis – injuries, suspects, that sort of thing. But it turns out his men were told to keep out of it. No sharing of reports. Nothing. A major in the military police – goes by the name of Tete Senyo – has the case and he's not letting anyone touch it. Then there's Eva's cousin Emmanuel. The one who's a judge in the supreme court. But I could only go to him if I had some really solid evidence. I feel as if we're caught in a catch 22. Without pathology results we're only guessing about Louis' injuries and how he died, so we're working in the dark. But I need to know more about that before I could use Emmanuel to help us get that information. Even then we're counting on the fact that Louis' body is still in Lomé.

Takashi hadn't thought about that possibility. He jogged along lost in thought for a few minutes then made up his mind.

— I think the body will be in the morgue, he said finally. There's one thing that stands out: whoever killed Louis and however he was killed, they went to some trouble to make it look like a gang killing. If Louis' body just disappeared – was dumped at sea, for example – that's going to point straight to the military or the government. They're the same thing. I think you said this Major Tete fellow is a gendarme so he'll have military backing. But it doesn't mean that he's necessarily acting for the government. He could be acting for a relation, colleague, friend – you know how it is.

Marius knew only too well. A lot of the police and

gendarmes were decent and honest, but there was an element who abused their power for all sorts of reasons.

— If it wasn't the machete wounds that killed him, but something else – a bullet or a beating are two things that spring to mind – wouldn't they want to get rid of the body so no one could examine it?

— We can't rule that out. But from what those soldiers were saying the machete had been used pretty extensively.

Marius turned sharply towards Takashi, his face screwed up in disgust. Takashi was apologetic.

— Sorry. I didn't want to say too much in front of the others. But apparently that's how it was.

Marius could feel sweat dribbling down his back. When he reached back to wipe it with his T-shirt he realised it was soaked through. No point looking at his watch again. They couldn't be far away from the lagoon.

— Let's get back to Kodjo and the car, he suggested. Can you tell me any more about that?

Takashi pictured the scene as Kwame and Ama had described it. The full moon, Kodjo standing in the grove of palm trees, the car with its headlights off, Kodjo's chest torn to pieces by bullet wounds.

— According to Kwame, it looked like a drive-by shooting. Someone in the car must have had a gun handy. Someone used to using guns, judging by how fast it happened. And who carries guns here? Soldiers, gendarmes, police. But also mercenaries and there are plenty of them in Lomé.

Marius agreed. In a place like Lomé it was too likely that the military was responsible for the deaths, but Takashi was right. Lomé was an easy place to pick up a mercenary, especially now. Thrown into the usual local mix were some tough looking soldiers from Burkino Faso that he'd seen around in the last week or so. Back-up in case of trouble during the elections, he guessed. He thought about the sort of gun that could have caused that sort of injury. Not just any old pistol by the sounds of it. Some sort of semi-automatic, probably a Glock that seemed to be Austria's only export to Togo. And there was no chance at all of having tests done on the bullets. It was as if they were working with their hands tied behind their backs.

— The way things stand, identifying the car is our best hope. I guess I could get Jojo to have another chat with his cousin at de Brujin's place. The car that was used must have picked up plenty of grass seed and maybe even scratches from that single track road you were describing.

But he didn't feel optimistic. It was too easy to wash down a car. Still…

Marius was getting tired – he really should get out for a run during the week. The main group of runners had crossed the road in front of Al Donald's and was heading east. Clouds that had been hanging around earlier had lifted and the sun was shining directly in his face. Well at least it meant they weren't far from the Laguna and a cold beer.

Ten minutes later there was the unmistakable smell of stagnant water, then the lower reaches of the lagoon came into sight. The bunch of runners took a left turn and headed down the Avenue François Mitterrand, back to the beach. Marius and Takashi stopped and waited until a few stragglers had passed them, then walked along a track that followed the edge of the lagoon. As they walked the water in the lagoon deepened and the rotting vegetation smell disappeared. Five minutes later and they arrived at the spot they were heading for, where some wooden benches and stools had been set out under the shade of a woven palm leaf shelter.

Marius went in to order some beer and Takashi wandered over to the side of the lagoon. He tried to ignore the rubbish caught in the reeds around the edges and looked at the cheerful pink and white flowers that seemed to float on the huge lily pads. They reminded him of summers in Hirakata when his parents would take him to see the lotus pond in the park. And he thought how typical it was of Togo; the occasional unexpected pockets of beauty that you found in amongst the clutter. He walked back and sat opposite Marius. The bottle of beer was frosty cold and Takashi held it against his cheek for a minute before taking a sip, glad to take some of the heat out of his face.

— What's this shooting that Mimi was telling me about? Do you think it's connected with Louis?

Marius took a few sips of his beer before he replied. He didn't know what to think.

— It might be. The shooting seems to have happened around about the time that Louis was talking to Lillian. Louis didn't meet up with his friends. I can't see any necessary connection, but it's a coincidence. I'm not ruling it out. Tomorrow I'm meeting up with a chap who might be able to tell me more about it. If it turns out to be another drive-by shooting then it would be even more of a coincidence. Mimi was right to think it could be important.

Takashi nodded then smiled.

— And how's her singing?

— You haven't heard her sing?

Takashi shook his head.

— She doesn't sing in front of me. I think she feels a bit awkward because of her mother. Maybe that's why she didn't start singing until the last year or so. You know, she felt a bit – I don't know how to say it – maybe the memories were too sad, you know, Miki being shot while she was singing. Anyway, it was when she started lessons with Mibou that I realised that she was serious about singing. And jazz. Just like Miki. He smiled.

— You have to come to the Spot next Friday – you'll be amazed. Mimi's a good singer. Really very good. She gets nervous but it doesn't show at all. Her voice is so deep and full. Marius had a sudden thought. Like Miki?

Takashi nodded and gave a little laugh at the memory.

— Sounds just the same. I'll work something out so I can get to the Sp'ot. Anyway, back to Kodjo and the car. Do the letters 'Gi' suggest anything to you?

Marius shook his head.

— No idea. Could be a motto. What are some words that might start with Gi – give, girl, gift – nothing rings a bell. Could be an ad I suppose: Gin – Gilbert. A football team? How about you?

— Same. Since Saturday I've been looking at all the cars to see what they've got on their bumpers but I haven't seen anything that starts with Gi – or Yi, for that matter.

— That's about all we can do. And keep thinking. At least I'll check de Brujin's car. I wish I could rule him out or in. But even if his car's clear, what's to say he didn't use someone else's.

Takashi looked at his watch.

I've got to get back to Chez Miki. But if there's anything else I can do…

— Nothing I can think of. Just be careful. And make sure nobody else knows what Ama saw. I feel as if we're almost on to something but if there's the slightest hint that we know — you know what it's like. Already there are too many of us who know about it for my liking, and even if we don't know as much as we want to, others might not realise that. But if we don't use our phones and if we meet up in secure places we should be okay.

A couple of men came along the path and sat at the table next to them. Marius stopped talking. He exchanged a look with Takashi that said 'let's go' and they finished their beer and walked up the road to where they could catch moto-taxis.

After the heat of the run, Marius enjoyed the feeling of

the wind on his face. He watched the back of the cars as they passed them on the road. There were quite a few eperviers[1] football stickers and one that made him laugh. It said All the parts falling off this car are of the best French craftsmanship. Quite a few had a 'D' for Germany where so many of the secondhand cars came from. He couldn't think of any European country that started with Gi, or Yi, but it was worth thinking about.

---

1 *Eperviers* is the nickname for the Togo national football team.

12

Marius wondered how safe this place was for the meeting with
Jacques. He looked around. In front of him was a full sized
swimming pool. The sun was making artistic honeycomb
patterns of light in the clear blue water but the air smelled
strongly of chlorine and Marius was happy to sit and watch.
A couple of young women were doing laps, breast stroking
slowly and chatting at the same time. At the shallow end the
water flowed into a lighter blue wading pool. Two little girls
in matching pink and blue swimsuits were bossing around a
younger boy in a red sunhat who was yelling his grievance
and trying to splash them back. Over the other side of the
pool was a bar where a few people were eating and drinking at
tables under Stella Artois umbrellas. A group of students from
the Lomé International Community School – LICS, everyone
called it – were standing by the bar jostling each other as they
waited for their hamburger orders to be filled.

It had been Mimi's idea to meet here and she'd organised
a pass for him. Jacques was already a member. Marius had
arrived early, a habit he still had from his Russia days. He felt
it gave him an advantage; time to position himself and check
things out. The thatch-roofed gazebo he'd chosen to sit in
was behind a row of blue-cushioned deck chairs that were
carefully lined up on the concrete surrounds of the pool.
There seemed to be far more uniformed workers than there

were jobs to do, though Marius was still waiting for his beer to arrive. Some of them were clipping bushes and raking the ground and then there were others who just seemed to be hangers on, perhaps making the most of having a relative working at the Club. One of them was behind Marius using a long stick with a hook to get mangos from the high branches of the trees behind him. But it all looked innocent enough and wherever you were, even out in the bush, there were always people around.

He was looking forward to meeting Jacques. Optimistic. Since the run yesterday he hadn't really thought about Louis. A succession of people had called in to the house in the afternoon, some of them friends, others locals with a problem. There were some people in his neighbourhood who seemed to treat him as a sort of village chief; someone who would arbitrate their disputes. Usually he didn't mind – it gave him a bit of insight into human nature – but yesterday it had got a bit much.

Even this morning Eva's brother had called in and stayed nearly all morning. He'd talked books and philosophy for an hour or so before leading the conversation round to what Marius assumed was the real reason for the visit. A certain person at the university was pinching his ideas – what was the best thing to do? How best to handle it? And so on. Marius was glad he hadn't continued with his idea of being an academic. All that talk, those words, that petty rivalry would take away his will to live.

The waiter arrived with his beer and his thoughts came back to the Club Tropicana. It was run by the school but doubled as a club for anyone who could afford the steep entrance fees. Annual membership only. Marius had heard talk about the connection between the school and the President and it made sense; a school run by foreigners could only stay in business if it suited him. What sort of compromises did they have to make? What about the army of workers in their brown jackets who seemed to be everywhere? Even in this expensive club – or maybe especially here – people were being watched. Marius was sure of it and that started him off again, worrying if it was a good idea to meet here.

According to Mimi, quite a few of the workers were making money on the side. Taking school property and selling it for profit was so common that the market people had a name for it: ce qu'lics. Pretty funny. LICS things. Marius' guess was that the ones doing the stealing were probably the informers as well and had some sort of 'special standing'. He looked around and started to count the number of workers that he thought were Kabyé. A bit rough he realised. Not every short stocky man had to be one of the President's tribe! He was definitely getting paranoid. He went back to watching the little kids splashing each other in the pool and let himself be entertained by their unthinking fun. Still, he was relieved when he saw Mimi and her friends arriving

Marius watched them walking around the top end of the pool. Mimi was holding the strap of a huge bag over her shoulder. It was bulging with books. She was saying something over her shoulder to Sarah and a tall slender man with close-cropped hair. It must be Jacques. Marius liked the look of him. He was laughing at whatever Mimi had said and he looked relaxed and comfortable with himself. No signs of the self-importance that sometimes went with the position of doctor. Or worse, the 'cat that ate the cream' look of a certain type of local man who made a living out of scamming European women.

It took a few minutes for them to sit down and go through the introductions. Closer up Marius could see that Jacques was older than he had thought. It must have been his day off because he was casually dressed in white T-shirt, chinos and brown leather sandals. Orders were placed for drinks and French fries. Marius had remembered he was supposed to be writing an article and he'd brought along a small spiral notebook that he thought a journalist might use. He wasn't really happy with the deception but he felt it would be too risky to let anyone else know why he was so interested. He took the pen and notebook out of his back pocket, flipped it open and scribbled the date at the top. Then he sat back and looked at Jacques, pen in hand.

— Very good of you to meet me. Do you mind if I take some notes?

— No. Take notes if you want. But of course no names.

— Of course not. Marius looked around. How do you feel about talking here? Do you think it's secure enough?

Jacques shrugged and smiled.

— As good as anywhere. So. Sarah tells me you're interested in finding out some more about the incident at the rally.

— That's it. I only know what I've heard from Sarah. There was shooting into the crowd and some people on the ground. Sarah thought you might have some more details – injuries, deaths. Place and time. Maybe even some idea about where the shots came from. Who might have done it. Something that would give some meat to the article. He regretted the choice of word but continued. A few facts. Marius was enjoying his new persona. Maybe he should think about a career as a journalist.

A waiter arrived with drinks and food and Jacques waited until he'd gone before he started talking.

— Sarah and I talked about the time and I agree with her; it was very close to 5 o'clock. Not that it matters. But don't worry, I know what you journalists are like. You've got to get the facts right. One thing I can tell you is more or less where the shooting happened. It was just after we'd got to the end of the Presidential Palace. You know where the wall ends, there's a street that goes across – no idea what it's called. It's the main drag that goes up to the stadium. I'm guessing it was either that road or it could have been the next one along. They both go straight to the Ghana border.

Marius wrote it down in his notebook and Jacques took some French fries and washed them down with beer before he continued.

— So that's the when and the where. I'm still not one hundred percent clear about what happened, but like Sarah said, we all heard these loud bangs. I knew straight away they were shots and my first thought was that it was going to be a repeat of 1999. He shook his head and half-smiled ruefully. How stupid was I to think that things would ever change. Anyway, I stopped straight away and looked towards where I thought the shots had come from. I'm pretty tall, so I could see over the heads of the others.

— Any idea who did it?

— There was a car heading up the road away from us. Not sure why but I feel fairly sure that's where the shots came from. But that's about it. I kept pushing through the crowd until I got to the front and then I saw people lying on the ground and blood all over the place.

— How many were shot?

— Well, I as far as I know it was four, but there could have been others who had superficial wounds that I didn't see. It was all a bit chaotic.

— Could you do anything for them?

— Not much. There was a man bleeding from his arm but some others were helping him so I checked the people lying on the ground. Two of them were men and I only had to look at them to see that it was too late: they were already dead, though of course I checked to make sure. The other was a woman in a really bad way – she'd been shot in the back.

Jacques stopped and shook his head, clearly upset by the whole thing.

— She was groaning and asking someone to help her.

There was a woman there – it's terrible, I still don't know her name. Anyway, she looked as if she was an organising type, so I asked her to get a taxi. She was great – probably saved the woman's life. She ran down to the main road that goes up to the border and grabbed the first taxi she saw. Told the passengers to get out, hopped into the passenger seat then made the driver come right up alongside us. We put the injured woman and man who'd been shot in the arm into the taxi and sent them off to the hospital. The woman went with them – that's why I didn't get her name. It sounds terrible, but there really wasn't anything we could do for the two men who had been killed. A couple of women had taken off their spare pagna and put them over the bodies but it still looked gruesome with the blood soaking through the cloth. There was nothing else I could do so I caught up with Sarah and Jenny. I passed word up the line about what had happened so everyone knew by the time we got to the stadium where the rally ended.

Marius was thinking about the car that Jacques had seen driving up the road. The way he described it, the road could easily have been the one that Louis had been walking down. If Jacques was right and the shots had come from the car it all linked up. He wanted to go there right now and test it out. The wall at the end of the Presidential Palace was a good starting point.

Jacques was talking about how the leader of the rally had used the deaths of the three people to whip up the crowd. Marius realised that was probably the intention of the shootings; stir up unrest, goad opposition supporters to go on the attack then come down heavy on everyone with curfews, make it seem as if the President's party was the only one capable of keeping order.

— Do you think there'll be retaliations? Marius thought he knew the answer.

Jacques bit his bottom lip, looked worried and nodded.

— Unfortunately. Some of the young men who support the opposition are too much like the RPT militia. They were warned against using violence but I wonder how much notice they take. Not much, is what I think.

— You mentioned that you saw a car. What made you think the shots came from there?

— Partly just the fact it was on the scene. I didn't see anyone shooting. But it was also the erratic way they were driving. The back was drifting out as if they'd just done a sharp turn too fast. It seemed to have swung across to the wrong side of the road as well.

Marius pictured the car – tried to remember what those streets were like. He thought there was a small lane that linked the road with a wider one parallel to it. That area was relatively new and laid out in a grid, not like the older suburbs which were really villages that had gradually grown together to make a city. It was too much to hope, but he asked anyway.

— Was there anything about the car that might suggest who it was?

Jacques looked disappointed and shook his head slowly.

— No. It was just a car.

— How about the make? Colour? Even that could give us a clue.

— I'm pretty sure it was a sort of greyish colour.

— Saloon? SUV?

— Just a saloon car. Looked a bit flash and new. Maybe an Audi or Volvo – even a Merc. Something like that. But as to who? No idea.

Jacques stopped and thought for a minute.

— Well no precise idea. But the way those people were shot! They were sprayed with bullets. A typical cowardly drive-by shooting. Of course it was the RPT. Could even have been military in a civvy car. You only have to think back to rallies in the past. It's not hard to know who to blame, but as for any accountability – chickens have teeth!

Jacques stopped talking and leaned back in his chair. He looked upset and took a few sips of his beer.

Marius didn't want to get carried away, but it was very interesting that the car was grey. And that it was a drive-by style of shooting. Just like Kodjo. He heard Mimi take a breath as if she was about to say something. Please, Marius thought silently, nothing about Kodjo. But she caught herself in time. Instead she took a few French fries, dipped them in a bowl of ketchup and nibbled on them. Then she wiped her hands on the paper napkin and turned to Jacques.

— There's a lot of that going on right now. Every day I hear another story from someone in the school about how they've been beaten up. Some people seem to be targeted more than others – the Ghanaians for example and even the Germans. Their drivers that is. Apparently they said something in support of the opposition. What a sick idea of democracy. But it keeps Europe happy. And because Togo turns a blind eye to the guns that pass through this country, nobody cares if a few Togolese people get killed or beaten up. Or thrown into prison.

Jacques agreed with her.

— You're right. It's the same thing every time the government feels even slightly challenged. It's not as if the rally was doing any more than showing peaceful opposition. Our lives are worth nothing here. Imagine if that happened in Paris or Berlin.

Marius could hear the depth of bitterness and admired Jacques for still caring and still trying to do something about it. He knew he'd become resigned and cynical and felt it acutely listening to Mimi and Jacques. He really should try to do more. At least he would write the article. He made a few notes in the notebook then closed it and put it on the table with his pen.

— I've got enough for the story. It was good of you to come and talk to me. Oh – just one thing. Do you know which hospital the woman took the two wounded people to?

— It was the Tokoin National; they have the best trauma unit there. But be careful who you talk to. Jacques looked thoughtful for a moment, then he took his paper napkin, smoothed it out and took a pen out of his top pocket. He wrote some names on it and handed it to Marius. Ask these people. They should be able to help and you can trust them.

— Thanks. Marius picked up the paper and looked at the names, then he folded it carefully and put it in his back pocket with the notebook.

He could see the others were happy to sit around and drink for a while. Jacques had cheered up and he and Sarah and Mimi were laughing at something Sarah had said. Marius drank down the last of his beer in one go then pushed his chair back and stood up.

— Permission to fall out, he said, and gave an ironic half salute.

Mimi laughed.

— Not even one more beer?

Marius patted his back pocket.

— Things to do. He leaned across the table and shook Jacques' hand. No – don't get up. Thank you, thank you. You've been more help than you can imagine. He turned to Sarah. And you too my dear. Maybe I'll see you at the Spot again?

Two hours later Marius pushed open the heavy glass doors at the entrance to the Tokoin National Hospital and took a couple of grateful breaths of fresh air. It was dark and the ground was wet from rain that had fallen while he'd been inside. It hadn't been easy but he managed to talk to one of the doctors from the list Jacques had given him. They were still fighting to save the life of the critically injured woman.

She was in intensive care but Dr da Silva had ignored protocol and taken Marius to see her. Her face was untouched, but she looked white and helpless, half covered by the big oxygen mask and hooked up to a machine with blinking lights and tubes that hung from a metal stand. Her husband and two boys around the age of Dzigi were sitting quietly in the waiting room. Dr da Silva said they were hoping that the sound of the children's voices might bring her out of the coma she'd been in for two days now. And what was Marius' blood type? Would he be able to give blood? They'd need some more for her soon. At least Marius had been able to do that.

Jojo was waiting for him in the car just up the road from the hospital gates. Marius greeted him and climbed into the passenger seat. Before he closed the door he leaned down and felt around for the cashew brandy. He slammed the door shut then unscrewed the cap and took a couple of mouthfuls, savouring the smooth, almost sweet taste, and the warmth in his throat and chest.

Jojo started the car first go and sat with the engine idling, not saying anything.

Marius put the cap back on the brandy and tucked it between his legs. Monday night. Mibou and Lucien would be playing at Chez Miki this evening. He wanted to talk over what he'd found out this afternoon, run it past Takashi and the others, see what ideas they had. But he was torn. Eva was expecting him for dinner and of course Dzigi too. In one way it would be easier to go home and forget about it for a while. But in an another way he felt that he didn't have a choice; something was driving him.

— Let's go to Chez Miki, he said to Jojo. Decision made.

Jojo negotiated the evening traffic in his slow, reliable way but he radiated silent disapproval. Marius thought about the hospital. He still wasn't entirely sure why he'd decided to go there. By all means he could use the information in the article that he really was going to write. But more than that, something of Jacques' anger had connected with him. In the instant that Jacques had mentioned the grey car some of the pieces had started to fall into place. He was going to find that car, not just for Louis but for Kodjo and for that woman and her family. Not to mention the two men who'd been killed at the rally. Marius took small sips of the brandy and laughed at himself. Marius the avenger!

He called Eva and told her he'd decided to take in some jazz at Chez Miki, then said goodnight to Dzigi. They were both okay about it, but he could tell that Dzigi really wanted him to be there. He would have loved to be able to tell them the real reason why he wouldn't be home but that would be crazy. If they didn't know what he was doing, there was less chance they'd come to any harm if things started to go wrong. How could he even think like that? If he thought anything could happen to them, surely he should just drop it all now.

He had to admit to himself there was another reason he didn't want Eva to know. She ran her own conveyancing business and was practical and pragmatic. Marius knew she'd tell him to stop playing games, accept things and move on. Growing up in the shadow of a dictator had that effect.

In lots of ways she was right, but much as he could acknowledge that, he knew there was no way he was going to let it go until he'd finished what he'd started. He felt obliged because no one else was going to do it. Then there were Mibou and Lucien and Takashi and Mimi – they were relying on him.

It was something he understood about himself without analysing it too closely; that he could get results in a way that others couldn't. He'd been taking on causes ever since he could remember. He thought of the ten-year-old boy – him and not him – who had earnestly tried to track down the thieves who stole his father's television set. And he recognised the same obsession now, though that village, that time, seemed like another world, and he a different person. It was easier not to think about any of that. He took another sip of the brandy and relaxed into the comforting inner warmth it gave.

13

When Jojo bumped the Toyota over the hard edge of the road and pulled up in front of the red and black lights of Chez Miki Marius tucked the brandy under the seat and made another decision.

— Take yourself back home Jojo. I'll get a taxi back.

Jojo looked grateful. He probably hadn't eaten, Marius thought, and there was no way he could be persuaded to eat with Takashi and the others. Best all round that he get back to the house, and Eva could probably do with a hand. He watched Jojo pull out into the traffic then he turned his back on the road and made his way into Chez Miki over the granite stepping stones.

Takashi was leaning on the bar talking to Yao, and Marius joined them. He saw Mibou and Lucien over the other side of the room setting up the keyboard. There were a few familiar faces; it seemed Le Grand Duo already had a following.

— Perfect timing for a bite to eat, Takashi said. I'm just organising it with Yao. Fish today – Japanese style. I've picked up some barracuda from Kweku. Kodjo's father, he added, as he saw Marius look blank.

— Splendid. Thank you. That poor man. How's he doing.

— He seems okay but you can see he's hurting. And he's angry. You know, that Kodjo was shot as if he was an animal and the police aren't doing a thing. Anyway, what will you have to drink?

112

— Asahi, definitely Asahi.

— Why don't you go on over, Takashi said, indicating with his head the comfortable chairs that fronted on to the garden. Looks like Mibou and Lucien are just about finished and Mimi won't be long.

Marius greeted a few acquaintances as he wandered over, then settled himself on the couch that looked over the garden. He relaxed into the soft cushions and realised that he was back in the same place he'd been last Monday night. The garden lights were making warm pools of orange in the darkness. Clouds that had been around earlier in the day had lifted and Marius looked up at the clear sky. The three stars of Orion's belt were directly overhead and he could make out the smaller stars of the sword. It had been quite a week. He thought of the line from Hardy that had seemed so suggestive, though he hadn't known why. Now it had more meaning. Twice no one dies. Hardy was intending to give comfort – once you're dead you're dead. But when Marius thought about Louis, it was as if he almost did die twice.

He felt certain that Louis must have witnessed something and that's why he never made it to the Rue des Bars; why his friends couldn't find him in town that night. And Kodjo had witnessed someone and had been shot for it. If Takashi was right and the grey car was coming back from dumping Louis on the beach then Marius felt pretty certain that Louis would have been dead before they put him in the car. For one thing they couldn't risk making noise at that time of the night in that spot. Then there was the characteristic drive-by shooting, at the rally and again in Agkamé. In Marius' experience killers tended to stick to the same method.

But what did Louis see? The same car that Jacques saw? Possibly. But to disappear as a consequence, surely it must have been someone he recognised. At that point Marius was stuck for any plausible theory. Louis was from Benin. He was a musician. Who could he possibly know who would shoot into a crowd of ordinary people?

— Hey Marius. How've you been?

Lucien had thrown his sticks on the ground and pulled himself on to the couch next to Marius with an athletic swing. Marius was relieved to be taken out of his thoughts. He'd reached a deadend. So to speak. He flinched inwardly.

Lucien and Mibou were joking around about one of the local musicians and Mibou came and pulled up a chair next to Marius.

— Attends! Attends! He said and the two of them laughed uncontrollably. They were trying to explain the joke to Marius when Takashi and Mimi came over carrying big square plates of chargrilled fish smelling of burnt soy sauce and ginger. Yao added some beer and a small ceramic flask of sake with tiny matching cups. They had nearly finished the tilapia when Mibou's phone rang. He checked the number – no name.

— Overseas! He said in a loud whisper to the others and pushed the answer button.

— Ciao Mibou. Lillian's voice sounded loud and the others had recognised it before Mibou mouthed 'Lillian' to them.

— Ciao Lillian. Comment?

— So so. What's happening over there?

— Nothing much. Toujours la même chose. Lucien and I are playing at Chez Miki tonight. Le Grand Duo. He laughed.

— Who? You and Lucien?

— That's it. We're all here. Mibou held the phone away from his ear so Lillian could hear the others.

— Mibou. There was a pause. Lillian started to say something then changed her words and started again. Mibou, I've been thinking a lot about that last phone call with Louis.

Marius could hear what she was saying and his immediate thought was that he should talk to Lillian himself. After the things he'd found out today he was even more convinced that whatever happened to Louis took place around 5 o'clock, the time of the phone call. He gestured to Mibou, pointing to himself and raising his eyebrows in a question. Mibou nodded to him and spoke into the phone.

— Just a minute Lillian. Here's Marius.

Marius took the phone and held it out from his ear so the others could hear.

— Hello Lillian. It's good to hear your voice. He meant it – he missed Lillian's lively presence in Lomé. We've found out more since you were talking to Mibou. It looks now as if something happened to Louis just after he was talking to you. We're getting a lot closer to working out who might have killed him, so anything you can tell us could be really important.

There was crackling on the line and Lillian's voice kept cutting out then coming back again. Marius put the phone closer to his ear.

— Can you say that again Lillian. I couldn't hear properly.

— Is this better? I was saying that I remember Louis said he was going to jam with Alex's band at the Mandingue. Then it seemed like he'd seen something really surprising. I'm pretty sure he said something like 'incroyable'.

— That's a lot better. Did you say incroyable?

— Oui. And of course I asked him what was so amazing.

— And?

— And he didn't really answer. He said something like 'mauvais' or it could have been 'le mauvais'…but suddenly the line was cut off, as if he just hung up. Why would he do that?

— Yes. Why. Are you sure it was mauvais? Could it have been mauvaise?

— No. I'm fairly sure it was 'mauvais', or 'le mauvais', as if it was some bad thing or person. I immediately thought of a man. Like a bad driver. Louis was walking down the road and I'm sure I could hear a car.

— A car? You're sure? That would fit with what we're starting to realise; that someone in a grey car could be responsible for Louis' death. Marius thought it easier not to tell Lillian about the rally yet.

— A hit and run?

— Not sure. Not yet. There's not much to go on and we're not getting any help as you can imagine, but we'll keep trying. When are you coming back? Lomé isn't the same without you.

It was good to hear Lillian's exuberant laugh down the phone.

— In a week or so. Philippe says he's sick of being by himself.

— Ciao Lillian Thanks. Here's Mibou again.

Marius handed the phone back and helped himself to some more fish. While Mibou was chatting with Lillian, Marius went over what she'd just told him. Knowing where Louis was planning to go that night wasn't going to help them because it was certain that he'd never reached there. And what did those two words tell them? That he saw something 'amazing' and 'bad'? On the one hand Lillian had definitely heard a car and that fitted with the theory that he and Takashi both felt fairly sure about. It all hinged on the grey car. But whose car, that was the question. He felt very uneasy about having said so much over the phone – Lillian could easily be a target for phone tapping because of Philippe – but on balance Marius thought it was probably better to have the information, scant though it was. Maybe the others could make some sense of it.

Mibou finished the call with Lillian. More sake and beer was poured and the last of the fish eaten. No one said much for a minute or two then Lucien waded in with his usual bluntness.

— Well Marius. Come on. What's happening? Fill us in 007! He laughed at his joke and Mibou joined in. Marius smiled and shared with them what he and Takashi had managed to find out so far. They already knew about Kodjo but not about the car and the rally.

— So you see, Marius finished. What Lillian just told us about hearing a car fits in with our theory: that they both saw the grey car and the men in it. The car that Jacques saw driving away from the rally; the one that Kodjo saw; the one that Ama saw. What we know about the car isn't much. It's a silver grey, newish saloon with some lettering on the bumper bar – probably a sticker. The letters could be a capital G or Y followed by an i. Ring any bells?

Marius stopped talking and looked at Mibou and Lucien, eyebrows raised, head slightly to one side.

— What about Lillian's husband? Mibou asked. Doesn't he have a car something like that?

Marius nodded. He wondered why he was so reluctant to believe that Philippe de Brujin was responsible for the killings. Was it because of Lillian? Because Philippe was European? But why would Philippe be taking shots at people in a rally? That bit of it didn't make sense.

— You're right of course. His is more of a metallic grey, but Philippe was out in it on the night of the murder. I don't know what he would have been doing shooting at people in a rally but I sent Jojo round to the de Brujn house last night. Did you know his cousin works as a night watchman there? Jojo asked him to check out things like a bumper sticker, or grass caught under the car from the track down to the beach. The car wasn't there when he called round but the cousin's going to have a good look for us.

Takashi checked his watch.

— Ten minutes to go, he said to Mibou and Lucien. But before you start playing, while we're all together, I just wanted to mention something. I'm sure you know as well as I do that outside the five of us – seven including Kwame and Ama – no one must know what we're trying to do. I'm already worried about that phone call. Not much we can do about it now. Whoever we're looking for has already killed four people. It could be five if they can't save the woman who's in intensive care. If that person or those people get to know even a hint of what we've found out we might get the same treatment, even though we don't know as much as they think we do.

Marius thought Mibou looked uncomfortable. Maybe he was just worried. But Marius hoped it wasn't something else. Had he said something? Marius knew that Mibou didn't have a bad bone in his body but he could be…what was it exactly? Erratic? Overly expansive? Especially when he was drinking whisky. In some ways he was trusting like a child, despite the street smart knowledge he'd picked up knocking around West Africa. Marius felt a churning of worry in his chest and took a few mouthfuls of beer. He didn't want to say anything. And it was probably nothing. Just his imagination.

Mibou gave Lucien a nudge and led the way to where they'd set up their instruments. Lucien seemed to have noticed something too. He raised his eyebrows and exchanged a look with Marius. It was half humorous but only added to a faint feeling of foreboding.

When they started playing Marius relaxed a bit. They were improvising on some tunes that Lucien had brought back with him from Bamako in Mali where he'd worked with Salif Keita. There was one that Lucien announced as 'Keep my cow' that was really catchy, despite the odd name. The beer and sake helped too, though nothing could entirely shake a tiny gnawing of anxiety that had settled in his stomach.

Around eleven he took a taxi back to town. There were four people squashed into the back seat when the taxi stopped in front of Chez Miki, and Marius felt lucky to be able to take the place of the man who had been in the front passenger seat.

The road was nearly deserted but at least there was no curfew in place. He'd been lucky that a taxi had come along when it did. Apart from the dim headlights the road was dark and the windows in the houses along the road were dark too.

They'd been travelling for ten minutes or so when the driver hit the brakes and stopped at a temporary barrier. He hadn't seen the dark-faced soldiers in their grey and blue camouflage uniforms. They weren't in a friendly mood. Marius and the others were ordered out of the taxi. AK47s were swung around like toy guns and Marius hoped for all their sakes that the safety catches were on. Exaggerated claims were made about the dire state of the taxi driver's papers and loud threats were made to arrest him. They all had to hand over their cartes d'identite and the driver was pushed around a bit. Then some notes changed hands and they were back in the taxi and on their way again. There was a noise like a shot and they all jumped, but it was only the taxi backfiring.

Marius was the last to be dropped off and the driver added CFA2000 to the fare. He was too tired to be bothered haggling and handed the money over, just relieved to be back home. It was fairly routine, but roadblocks like that were always unsettling.

The house was in darkness when he let himself in through the laundry door. Curtains had been pulled over the one high window in the room and the door to the kitchen was closed. Marius found himself in total darkness as he closed and locked the door behind him. The light switch was on the other side of the room near the kitchen door and he took cautious slow steps in the pitch black. The laundry doubled as a storage room and he didn't want to collide with some box or basket and disturb the family. He felt as if he should be somewhere near the kitchen door and he reached out with his right hand, feeling for the laundry tubs that were just in front of the light switch. He couldn't feel anything – just empty space – and he felt a flutter of panic. He knew it was irrational, but he found total darkness disturbing, to the extent that it made him slightly nauseous.

Without warning he knocked the shin of his right leg on a sharp surface. It threw him off balance and reaching out to steady himself he felt the tops of bottles that clanked as he pushed himself upright again. Crates of empty bottles, he thought. He was planning to throw a party for Eva's birthday and Akosua had promised to send him some extras. It was an odd place to stack them though and he wondered who had put them here. He felt with his left hand to work out where the edge of the crates was and how to negotiate his way around them without knocking them over.

Going by touch he guessed that there were nine crates stacked in piles three high. The crates seemed to be blocking most of the passageway between the washing machine and the cupboards opposite. Now that his eyes were getting a bit used to the darkness Marius started to make out some vague shapes. He was right. There on his left was the smooth edge of the washing machine. He put his left hand on it then reached with his right hand for the edge of the crates to manoeuver his way through the gap.

He was expecting to feel the rough edge of a plastic crate. Instead he felt something quite different. It was soft and silky to touch but fleshy and alive. And moving. At the same time Marius sensed rather than saw a long coil like a hose. He snatched back his hand and rushed for where he now thought the light switch would be.

At first the light dazzled him and he opened and closed his eyes a few times to get back his sight. Then he saw the shiny grey scales of a black mamba that was slowly moving around the bottles in the middle of the crates. Its head was coming out of one of the openings in the plastic crate and its mouth was wide open. It was making a loud hissing sound. Marius could clearly see the telltale black lining inside the gaping mouth. There was a long moment when they looked at each other.

Now that he could see again Marius felt back in control and he watched the snake as it tried to work out where the danger was coming from. Gradually it stopped hissing and adjusted itself more comfortably around the bottles. There were coils on coils of smooth grey scales and Marius guessed that it must have been at least three metres long.

He decided the mamba would be happier in darkness and wished it a silent goodnight as he switched off the laundry light and let himself into the kitchen, closing the door behind him then switching on the light. The frame of the door fitted snugly and there was no way the snake could get through to any other part of the house. Marius guessed that it would settle down again anyway. It had seemed quite comfortable in the crates until he disturbed it.

Satisfied, he took a bottle of beer from the door of the fridge and took it through to the living room. The long French windows were letting in moonlight and he relaxed on to the couch, feet up on the arm rest at the end, a pile of cushions behind him. He sipped his beer from the bottle and thought about the snake.

The most urgent thing was how to get rid of it. That shouldn't be too hard. There was sure to be a snake handler somewhere in the neighbourhood. Jojo would know where to find him. More immediately, when should he warn the others? Should he wake them up now and tell them? For a minute he thought of waking Jojo and sending him for the snake handler right now but then decided against it. Everything could wait until the morning. If he woke Dzigi and Seri now they might be too sleepy to remember anything in the morning. He'd put a note on Eva's door. That would do it.

More disturbingly, what was the snake doing in the crates? An occasional black mamba showed up in the neighbourhood but they were usually after frogs. There were none of those around the house. And on top of that, the laundry door closed automatically and there were no holes in the ceiling or walls so it was unlikely that it found its own way into the laundry. In that case it must have been in the crates when they were brought from Le Jazz Spot. But that seemed just as improbable. It didn't make sense. And if he accepted that it was already in the crate, what was it doing at Le Jazz Spot? There were people going in and out of there all day.

Marius didn't like the idea that the snake could have been put there deliberately, but so far it seemed the strongest possibility. It was really staggering how many people still believed in the magic powers of snakes, and black mambas were favourites. Men turning themselves into snakes, snakes turning themselves into men for all sorts of reasons, none of them good. The thought of such idiotic beliefs depressed him. There were people he knew who believed that a juju man could use a black mamba to ruin a business. Reasonably well-educated people at that.

What if the mamba had been deliberately planted in Le Jazz Spot? That would mean that someone was targeting Mibou. Marius had to admit it was possible; he'd better warn Mibou and Akosua.

He finished the beer and took the empty bottle into the kitchen. Then he tore a page out of an exercise book lying on the table and found a marker pen in the drawer. For a couple of minutes he tried to think of what to write, but nothing came to mind that didn't sound like a joke. He'd just have to make sure he was up before everyone else. Then he had an even better idea. If he slept in front of the laundry door then no one could go through it without waking him up. Of course. He half carried, half dragged a fairly comfortable chair from the living room and put it in front of the laundry door, then he brought the ottoman in and settled back in the chair, feet stretched out. With his shoes lined up neatly on the floor next to the chair he switched off the light and started counting down from one hundred, but didn't get much beyond sixty before he was asleep.

14

When Marius woke up he had a feeling of being watched, and sure enough, three pairs of eyes were staring at him. He knew there was something he should remember and then it came flooding back to him. As he explained about the mamba in the laundry the eyes opened wider, especially Dzigi's. Seri had got as far away from the laundry door as she could and was standing against the living room wall, holding her school uniform bunched up in both hands, as if that would help if the snake appeared. But Dzigi wanted to see for himself and finally Eva and Marius gave in and let him have a peek. The snake was sleeping peacefully and didn't stir when the door was opened a crack, but Dzigi could see the looping coils and he was as frightened as he'd hoped to be.

It took almost the whole of Tuesday morning before the black mamba was safely removed from the laundry. When the last people had finally left Marius made himself a ginger tea and took it out onto the terrace. The air was hot and oppressive but there was just the faintest hint of a breeze and at least the bougainvillea over the lattice gave plenty of shade. He put his mug on the small cast iron table and then relaxed into the weathered old cane chair.

It was interesting, the talk he'd had with Moses the snake man. Apparently there was a good living to be made in the snake business. Moses had explained at length and more than once that the secret of handling snakes was to win their trust.

124

To do this he, Moses, only had to show he had no intention of hurting them. And that he had no fear that a snake would bite him. His thoughts towards them were kind and the snakes understood that. Marius had heard the same explanation from crocodile keepers in the Ivory Coast. He didn't think he should mention to Moses the recent incident in Yamoussoukro where a keeper who had fed and tended crocodiles in the palace moat for nearly fifty years became a meal for a crocodile who finally decided to eat him instead of a half dead chicken.

What interested Marius more was that Moses was of the opinion that the mamba was probably bespoke! What a bizarre thing, to deliberately raise a mamba to hibernate in a crate. But apparently that's what some of the snake handlers did, and the clients bought the crate with the snake.

Moses dismissed the idea that the snake would have accidentally found its own way into either the bar or the house. Of course he stressed that he, Moses, would never do such a thing – his only concern was to look after the snakes – but there were other snake men around and not too far from here who made plenty of money by breeding mambas for bad juju. Marius wanted to believe that Moses was not one of those and that the snakes would continue to respect his kindly intentions.

Most households had stacks of these crates of empty bottles – not just of beer but sodas and colas and just about every other sort of drink. It would be easy to come and go with empty crates and no questions asked. The place where the snake in its crate was planted could have been, and probably was, in the bar of Le Jazz Spot. In that case it was someone wanting to use the snake to get at Mibou, just as Marius had suspected. According to Moses, that would fit with a belief that had wide currency: that the presence of a black mamba would ruin a business. When you thought about it, Marius mused, there could be something feasible in that belief at a practical level, if not in a juju context.

Another possibility was that the person who brought the empties to his house had a grudge against Marius and put the snake in with the other crates. That would make it more plausible as to why the snake still seemed to be dormant until Marius put his hand on it. He grimaced involuntarily at the thought. One thing was for sure – he couldn't put off telling Akosua and Mibou any longer. He pulled out his phone and called Mibou and they arranged to meet at the Spot in the evening. Mibou was giving music lessons at the international school and then he had a lesson with Mimi at his house. Any time after that he'd be there. Marius would have preferred earlier but it would have to do.

It was after nine o'clock before Marius finally made it to the bar. Eva had gone out with some friends and it was Marius' turn to get Dzigi and Seri off to bed. Seri was no trouble but Dzigi was hyperactive. It was all about the snake: partly the excitement about what his friends had said and what he'd told the teacher, and partly hiding the fact that he was frightened. Marius had a hard time getting him to go to bed, let alone to sleep. In the end he told him a long story about the little people of the Russian forests and Dzigi finally settled down. Marius left Jojo guarding the downstairs area and realised it made him feel a lot better too. Much as he didn't want to admit it, he was still a bit jumpy.

He found Mibou and Mimi sitting at the table in the alcove under the old wisteria vine just to the left of the entrance of Le Jazz Spot. Mimi was laughing at something Mibou had just said and Marius could see they'd been enjoying a few drinks. There were some people at the tables in the garden and on the other side of them Akosua was chatting to a couple of locals who were sitting on the high stools at the bar. The breathy notes of Stan Getz were playing over the loudspeakers. Marius waved Akosua over, then sat down opposite Mimi and Mibou and greeted them.

Akosua came up at her usual slow pace and looked happy to see him. She'd decided that Marius would have a Star beer and had brought one over for him and another one for Mibou. As she took the glass and bottles off the tray she chatted to Marius.

— Mr Marius. How is the family?

— Well Akosua, they're not very happy with me right now. He laughed to show her it wasn't too serious.

— Why? What have you done this time? Last time it was the rabbits!

They both laughed and Marius reminded the others.

— I had a cunning plan to breed rabbits and sell them for meat but in the end I got too attached to them so one day I just let them out and they ate nearly all the flowers in the garden before moving on.

They all laughed.

— Was it rabbits again? Mimi asked.

— No. I learned my lesson. No, this time it was a snake.

— Why? Akosua asked. You're not planning to breed snakes now I hope?

— Nothing like that. Sit down for a minute Akosua, I want to tell you about it as well. She could see he suddenly looked serious so she put her tray on the table and sat down next to him.

Marius gave them a summary of the drama of the black mamba and told them about Moses and how he thought that the snake had been deliberately planted somewhere, probably in the bar. Akosua started to look more and more worried and she made dramatic sucking noises as Marius talked. He was still going over the possible scenarios when she interrupted him.

— I think I know when it happened Mr. Marius. To think I was that close to the snake and didn't even know. It must have been in the storeroom.

— I'm not surprised, Mibou said. That room is always so dark. I don't know how you find anything in there.

— Maybe we need a better light, Akosua said. She looked at Mibou more thoughtful than accusing. Anyway, I don't think the snake was there long. In fact now that I think about it, I'm pretty sure that it was only yesterday that the new crates were put in there.

Now we're getting somewhere Marius thought.

— Go on, he said.

— I thought it was strange at the time, she continued, but then it just went out of my mind. The thing is that when I came into work this morning I noticed something. She looked at Mibou. You know the first thing I do on Monday mornings is a weekly stocktake because the brewery delivery comes in the afternoon. When I went into the storeroom I could see that someone had added crates to that pile of spare empties. Not the ones that go back to the brewery but the discontinued stock that's been around for months. Patience was looking after the bar for me yesterday so I rang her to find out what was going on. She said that Bruno – Akosua gave a meaningful glance in Mibou's direction – had asked if he could store something in the back room so of course she said yes and didn't really give it a thought. Apparently he came with someone else and was in and out quickly. They didn't even stay for a drink.

The mention of Bruno's name gave Marius a bad feeling and he could see Mibou tense up as well. Mibou and Bruno had started out as partners in the bar but Bruno had almost succeeded in cheating Mibou out of his money plus his share in Le Jazz Spot. Bruno had tried some very dirty tricks and only a combination of legal threats and Françoise buying Bruno off had resolved it in the end. Nowadays Bruno acted as if nothing had happened but they all had good reason to mistrust him. Marius knew that Bruno was intensely jealous of Mibou. Bruno wanted to be a big musician and he hung around with some of the lesser musicians in Lomé but he couldn't forgive Mibou for his talent.

— Sorry Mr Mibou. I should have told you.

— Hey. Not your fault. Mibou's gravelly voice was friendly and he smiled at Akosua. How were you to know?

Akosua was relieved and went on.

— In the afternoon my cousin came round to pick up some crates for himself so I asked him to take the others to you Mr Marius. You know how you asked me for some spare ones for the party. I was glad to get rid of them to make more space for the brewery stuff.

Marius acknowledged his appreciation with a nod of his head and a smile.

— Thank you. Any reason he came yesterday and not any other time?

— He's been going to come round for ages. Then a friend of his with a truck came to visit so I'm sure that's why.

It sounded logical enough to Marius.

— Nothing suspicious there then. But Bruno! You know what he's like Mibou. He would be just the sort of person to hide a snake in your bar.

— Yeah. And try to put me out of business like he did before.

— But why now? Mimi asked.

Mibou shook his head. Akosua picked up the tray and stood up.

— I'd better get back to the customers – I'll let you know if anything happens.

— Or you might hear something, Marius suggested. But be careful.

She nodded and smiled at him.

— You too Mr Marius.

— So, back to the snake. Let's say that for whatever reason, it was deliberately planted in your storeroom with the hope that it would perform some sort of juju against you, Mibou.

— Okay.

Marius continued.

— It could just be a coincidence that it happened right now when we're trying to find who killed Louis. But let's say it's not. Let's say that there's a connection. What could it be?

— What we're all worried about, Mimi said. Whoever did it knows that we're trying to find out who they are.

— And maybe they think we're getting close, Mibou added.

— But why target Mibou? Mimi asked.

— There's the phone call with Lillian last night. That came through on Mibou's phone. Could there be anything else Mibou? Marius gave him a direct look. He remembered how uncomfortable Mibou had been out at Chez Miki. If there was something Mibou hadn't been saying it needed to be out in the open.

Mibou met his gaze for a second then looked down and took a deep breath. He gave a quick embarrassed glance at Mimi.

— Go on Mibou, she said and smiled at him. Don't worry about me.

— The thing is, I don't know. He sighed and lifted his shoulders and eyebrows in a 'you know what I'm like' look. There's a part of Saturday night that I just can't remember. I was at Sunrise and I'd been drinking whisky and god knows what else. I have a feeling I was talking about Louis but have no idea what I might have said. I don't even know how I got home.

Marius and Mimi both knew exactly what he would have been like.

— Okay, Marius said. So let's add to the phone call the fact that you might have said something at Sunrise. Any idea who might have heard you?

— Well, it was mostly musicians – you know how we like

to have spaghetti for breakfast at Sunrise. But it's a small place and there were people at the other tables. No idea who.

— Nothing to go on then?

Mibou shook his head.

— Nothing I can remember. Just the spaghetti. What about Bruno? He doesn't fit in at all.

— Could he have been at Sunrise?

— I suppose so. He goes there sometimes with those pseudo musos he hangs out with. Even if he was there and I said something, why would it worry him?

Mimi poured herself another glass of white wine then leaned down and pulled a notebook and a clear plastic case of miniature pens out of her bag. She flipped the notebook open and Mibou and Marius watched as she deftly outlined a little manga style cartoon figure.

— It's too hard to try to think of connections between all these things, she said. So I'm going to do a diagram.

Mibou laughed and Mimi gave him a stern look.

— That's how I think, she said. In pictures. She wrote 'Louis' next to the figure then drew another one and labelled it 'Kodjo' and drew a dotted line between them. She added four more little manga figures with 'rally' next to them. Another dotted line joined the rally to Louis then to Kodjo.

— And the grey car, Marius suggested.

— Right. She drew a little car heading along the dotted line between the rally and Louis.

Mibou admired the drawing.

— Hey! You've got hidden talents. Then he had a closer look. When you see it like that, he said, the people in that car almost certainly have to have something to do with the RPT. It could be military, gendarmes, militia, whatever. Why else would they want to shoot into an opposition rally?

Mimi wrote RPT on the car. Then she added a Gi in a round frame like a siren on top of the car.

— Mustn't forget that.

Marius picked up the notebook.

— Do you mind?

He held the drawing out to the light coming from the lamp behind them on the wall and looked at it thoughtfully. Then he put it back down in front of Mimi.

— So. If there is any connection between the snake and our investigation it would be between the car – because that connects all the deaths – and Mibou and Bruno.

Mimi drew a figure for Mibou and connected him with a line to Louis. She added a trumpet for Louis and a saxophone for Mibou. Then she drew a happy looking coiled snake with big eyes and another figure with Bruno next to it and connected them. She took her hand away and considered the drawing for a minute. Then as she talked she pointed to the different parts of her diagram.

— So if the snake is to scare Mibou or threaten him somehow and it's because of Louis, then if Bruno was the one who put the snake in the storeroom it means he would be connected to the RPT, if we're right about that. She looked at Mibou and Marius in turn. Do you know if he is. Connected with the RPT?

Mibou suddenly sat up straight and looked at some imaginary spot in the sky, thinking. He looked around as if he expected to see shadowy figures, then he leaned closer to Marius and Mimi and spoke in a low voice.

— The President's brother. I heard that Bruno was hanging out with Paulie. It was after we'd stopped talking to each other but someone told me about some big trip he went on up north. A military show of some sort I think it was. You know what Bruno's like. If he thinks he can get money out of someone he doesn't care how he does it or who it is. He's psycho. Mibou demonstrated by circling his hand around his ear a few times.

Marius felt worried. That would ramp up the danger level by a few notches.

— How sure are you Mibou?

— It was all hearsay but I remember now. It was Henri who told me. I trust him. He's not a bullshit artist like others I could name.

— If you're right, that's even worse than I imagined. Though I suppose, Marius went on, thinking aloud, it doesn't mean that Bruno is acting for him. What it does show though is that Bruno has – or has had – connections with the RPT.

— Yeah. Can't remember the details. Henri was telling it like a joke against Bruno, the way he was all dressed up like a big man and behaving like some sort of dictator.

Mimi carefully drew a red line between Bruno and the RPT car and between Bruno and Mibou. Then she changed the colour to green and drew one between Louis and Mibou.

Marius enjoyed watching her easy artistic lines and smiled at the red and green divide.

— What colour are you going to make the snake?

— Black. It's a black mamba. She laughed. Okay, I know they're really grey, but artistic licence!

Marius started to relax a bit. At least they were getting somewhere.

— This calls for another drink. Marius looked at Mibou's bottle. Empty. Then at Mimi's wine – plenty left. He caught Akosua's eye and held up two fingers.

Mimi looked at her watch.

— It's getting late. I have to work tomorrow. She pointed to the half-full bottle of wine. Can you ask Akosua to put the rest of this in the fridge for me. She closed the notebook, put it back in her large bag and stood up.

Will you get a chance to pass all this on to Takashi? Marius asked.

Sure. I'll do it as soon as I get home.

— Good. I'll be meeting up with him tomorrow and the more he knows the better. How are you getting home? Marius asked. Do you need a lift?

— It's not a problem. I'll catch a taxi. They all go past Chez Miki.

She gave Marius a kiss on each cheek and waved a finger at Mibou as if admonishing a child.

— Behave yourself, she said smiling.

Mibou raised his eyebrows and opened his eyes wide in pretend innocence, pointing speechlessly at himself.

— Moi? He asked, then laughed in the way he had that got everyone else laughing too.

— Chiao.

She lifted the black metal bar on the gate and heard it click behind her. The narrow sandy street was dark, but to her left she could see the lights on the main road. On either side of her, high walls hid the houses and compounds. Behind her Stan Getz was playing 'Night and Day' and Mimi hummed along with it. She walked slowly in the darkness feeling content and happy.

When she was almost at the junction with the main road, bright headlights swept around the corner into the lane. Mimi shielded her eyes with her hand and backed against the wall. The car went straight past, moving fast towards Le Jazz Spot. As the vehicle approached, the headlights had blinded her but now, watching the red taillights moving down the lane, she realised it was a military police truck. The small two-door variety with an open tray on the back. Mounted on the tray was a large automatic artillery gun. A gendarme was standing with one arm on the handle of the gun, leaning over the cabin of the truck, and Mimi watched as it stopped outside the Spot.

Her body went tight with fear. It wouldn't help to go back, so she walked the last few metres to the end of the lane. Soon she was squeezed in the back of a taxi with two elaborately dressed women with beautiful headscarves that seemed to fill the whole car. She was tempted to text or call Marius but her instinct told her to do nothing. What could they do after all?

Inside the Spot Akosua was checking some orders with Mibou. Marius waited at the table. There was no hurry. He rested the back of his head on his hands and stretched out his legs, enjoying the balmy night. Behind him the gate swung hard open. A large thickset man in camouflage shirt and trousers stood just to the right of him. His camouflage pants were tucked into black lace-up boots. A red beret was pulled forward on his head but didn't hide the dark brown spots that marked his face. His mouth was stretched tight and pulled down at the corners. He didn't look as if he'd come for the music. A second man came through the gate, wearing the same uniform and carrying a Kalashnikov. The few customers still in the Spot all looked up at them. Over the loudspeakers Stan Getz was playing 'The girl from Ipanema'.

Akosua took in the situation – she'd had visits like this before. Leaving Mibou at the bar she walked slowly up the path between the bushes and the low lights, her left shoulder dipping and rising as she walked.

— Good evening. Can I help you?

The large gendarme ignored her and looked around. His expression didn't change. Marius thought he was going to be in trouble, but the man pulled a piece of paper from the pocket of his jacket and unfolded it, taking his time. With a fat forefinger he pointed at a spot on the paper and showed it to Akosua.

— This man, was all he said.

Marius watched as Akosua led the two gendarmes along the path to where Mibou stood watching.

Marius admired the way she was dealing with the situation. She sounded quite normal as she spoke to Mibou and gestured towards the gendarmes.

— They're here to see you.

— Thanks Akosua. Mibou tried to look relaxed. How can
I help?

Polite cooperation was the only approach that had any
hope of working and Akosua and Mibou were working on it.
Marius would have felt more optimistic if he hadn't just got
the news about Bruno and Paulie.

— Papers!

Mibou pulled his wallet out of his back pocket and showed
his carte d'identite.

— Licence. Permits.

The gendarme in charge was about the same height as
Mibou but twice the width. He stood uncomfortably close and
Marius thought how slender and vulnerable Mibou looked.
What were they after? Money? Had they just happened to call
in here tonight? He thought not.

Mibou had turned away from the gendarmes and walked
behind the bar. He called Akosua over. She produced a key and
he used it to open a drawer under the counter. He pulled out
some loose papers, glanced at them then came out from behind
the bar. The large gendarme strode over towards him and pulled
the papers roughly out of his hands. Without looking he ripped
them in pieces and bits of paper fell on the ground in front of
him. He twisted them into the dirt with his large black boot.

— That's what I think of your papers.

He made a sign with his head and the second man strode
forward holding his gun with both hands. With a quick upward
movement he struck Mibou across the side of his face with
the butt of the Kalashnikov. Mibou was knocked sideways and
crashed into the stools at the bar. The two gendarmes turned
and walked out. They paid no attention to the few people who
were sitting at tables in the garden, or to Marius. The gate
slammed behind them. Marius heard the truck driving off as
he hurried to help Mibou.

Akosua and a customer had helped Mibou to his feet and on to a stool. Marius snatched up a tea towel that was on the sink behind the bar and put it under the cold water tap then squeezed it out and folded it to make a wad. Mibou held it against his face and Akosua went to get some ice from the freezer. Marius sat on a stool next to Mibou.

— That was quick. Sorry I couldn't do anything. I didn't see it coming at all. I thought they were just after a bit of drinking money.

Mibou tried to smile but it looked painful.

— Me too.

— My god that big guy is an ugly looking character.

Akosua came up with a bowl of ice cubes. She gently pulled the blood-soaked cloth from Mibou, put some ice cubes inside, then gave it back. She took his hand and positioned it so that the ice covered the lump that was already pushing out under the cut.

— Keep the pressure on it.

Mibou nodded and put his elbow on the counter and rested his head against the cloth.

Then Akosua went back behind the bar and took a bottle of whisky off the glass shelves on the wall behind the bar. She put it on the counter with two glasses.

— Thanks my dear, Marius said as he reached for the bottle. He filled both glasses and pushed one within easy reach of Mibou's free hand.

Then he leaned closer to Mibou and peered at the place around the wound.

— How are you feeling?

Mibou tried to laugh then winced.

— I've got a thick skull, lucky for me. He gulped down most of the whisky. That feels better.

The other customers were standing up getting ready to leave and Akosua went over to settle their bill. Muddy bits of paper were still lying on the ground and Marius pointed to them.

— Are these the only copies?

Mibou nodded. Marius took a couple of sips of his whisky then put the glass on the counter. He slid off the stool and bent over the scraps of paper. Some of them were untouched. The ugly dark pattern from the soles of the boot had marked some, but he could still see some print under the dirt. The bits that had been stamped into the ground were worst off. He picked up the scraps one piece at a time, held them at arm's length and gently shook each one to get rid of the loose sand and dirt. Akosua came over to help. She found an empty carton and after a few minutes most of the scraps were in the box.

Marius washed his hands at the tap behind the bar then climbed back onto the stool. Mibou just sat there holding the ice in the towel against his head. The small movements he made hurt too much so he sat very still, only the hand with the whisky glass moving.

— I think that was another warning, Marius said.

Mibou just shook his head. Marius could see it was all getting too much.

— Come on, let's get you home.

Marius helped him off the stool. The ice in the towel had started to melt and blood from the cut had turned the damp patches of the cloth a sickly looking red. Mibou looked at it in disgust. Marius took it from him, and holding it by the clean ends took it round to the sink behind the bar, rinsed it out, added some more ice cubes and gave it back to him. Mibou put it back up on his face and Marius picked up the bottle of whisky that was still on the counter.

— All set?

Akosua walked to the gate with them. Marius hoped she was as calm and in control as she appeared to be on the surface, but he was relieved to see her husband waiting in the car just outside the gate. Relieved but worried too.

— Akosua my dear. I wonder if you could keep this to yourself. This – he gestured towards Mibou still holding the cloth against his face – and the snake incident. I would really rather your husband didn't know. How do you feel about that?

Akosua put her hand on his arm.

— I'd rather it that way. She smiled. He might try to stop me working here. Now you be careful. Both of you.

— You too. Good night.

She closed the gate behind them. Back at the bar she ejected Stan Getz and replaced it with a CD of Fela Kuti's greatest hits. As she washed the glasses she bopped around a bit to the music and felt as if she was making a small personal protest.

On the other side of the wall Mibou and Marius were going over the events of the last couple of days. Marius was talking and Mibou was answering in monosyllables. He'd asked Marius to stay for a drink and their glasses were almost empty. Mibou had found some pain-killers in the medicine box and he'd taken four of them with the whisky.

They were sitting in the kitchen and he was holding a clean cloth and ice against his face. The bleeding had eased off and Marius had forced himself to have a good look at the cut when he helped change the cloth. The wound was open but not too deep. No stitches needed. As he suspected, the strike was more a jab than a full hit. Intended to humiliate, not to seriously wound.

— I wonder what's going to come next. We've got to get our hands on that car and the driver. Attack is the best means of defence.

Mibou just sat there looking dazed and Marius could see his eyelids drooping. He tossed down the last mouthful of whisky and pushed his chair back.

— I'm going to help you to your bedroom and then push off.

Mibou tried to smile.

— Like a baby.

— Come on. Are you right to get up?

Mibou nodded and pushed himself upright. He stood for a moment his head spinning, then Marius took his arm and walked him into the bedroom. Mibou kicked off his shoes and stretched out on the bed fully dressed.

— Anything else I can do?

Mibou pointed to a switch by the door.

— Fan.

Marius flicked the switch and the fan started to turn slowly, making a soft thud with each revolution.

— Goodnight.

— 'Night.

Marius switched off the light and let himself out the kitchen door, locking it behind him.

15

As Mibou struggled between sleep and consciousness he felt sure somebody was hitting him in the face. He could see the person quite clearly – a man in a camouflage uniform with long dreads and a djembe that he was using to hit him with. No one he knew. Then he opened his eyes and felt a sharp pain just below his left eye. It came back to him; the ugly gendarme stamping on the papers for Le Jazz Spot, the tall man rifle butting him in the face.

He cautiously touched the place that was hurting, screwing up his face as he did so. It didn't seem too bad. The lump felt quite big but when he looked at his hand there was no fresh blood. He'd fallen asleep holding the wet cloth against his face and as he sat up he could see it on the pillow. The cloth had dried out during the night and the ice had melted on to the pillowcase, leaving a water stain streaked with blood.

As he sat up his head started to throb so he stayed as he was on the side of the bed with his head down, waiting for the thumping to stop. When it did he stood up and wandered into the bathroom. He looked at himself in the mouldy mirror over the sink. His left eye had closed over and a purple and blue mark spread out from the lump. The gash under the lump was a good three or four inches long and moist with beads of blood forming in it. But Marius was right, he thought, as he moved his face closer to the mirror and peered at it. It wasn't very deep.

A shower would help. He adjusted the pressure to a soft trickle and stood under it for a long while, lifting his head slightly to let the water flow onto his injured face. As he stood there enjoying the feeling of the tepid water he tried to think clearly about what was going on.

For a start there was that snake. What if Dzigi or Seri had found it in the laundry? Or if Akosua had disturbed it in the storeroom? Mibou was skeptical of juju but of course he'd heard the stories and plenty of people he knew believed in it absolutely. If the black mamba had come out of its crate and into the bar who knew what wild ideas about witchcraft would have gone the rounds.

Then Mibou thought about Bruno. The only reason he would be hanging around was to make trouble. But what sort of trouble? Could Bruno have been at Sunrise? Anyway what difference did that make?

He turned off the shower and dried himself then checked his face again in the mirror over the sink, turning it back and forth and running his hand over his chin. No need to shave today.

If Françoise was here she'd have some ideas; she could always see through Bruno. In fact it was starting to remind him of years ago when he and Françoise had decided to start a jazz bar. At that time Bruno seemed to be his friend, perhaps his closest friend. It had taken Mibou a long time – too long – to realise what sort of person he really was. Françoise hated Bruno and was always asking Mibou why he hung out with him, but Mibou just couldn't see it.

It still amazed him how someone could be so good at pretending to be one sort of person and yet be someone entirely different. In the early days he and Françoise had rented this house and they'd started the bar in the big garden that came with it. Bruno had set it all up. He knew that Mibou had been wanting to own his own place. The hours they spent drinking and talking about it! It was Françoise who was paying the rent. Always collected by Bruno. To be helpful. At the time, neither of them realised that Bruno was taking half and giving the other half to the owner.

When they decided to buy, again it was Bruno who managed it all; the purchase, the builders for the bar. Françoise was always busy at work and Mibou had to admit to himself that he was useless about organising things. There'd always been someone around to do it for him – an older brother or sister, a friend. Françoise had told him that he'd never grown up, that he was still the little boy playing music and waiting for the applause that always came. He took it as a joke at the time, but looking back he could see she was right.

Anyway, the thing was to try to get back his memory of Saturday night. He wanted to help find whoever had killed Louis as much as the others but as usual he seemed to have fucked things up.

Antoinette had just arrived when he went out to the kitchen. She had her back to him and was lighting one of the gas rings. The kettle was already full and she put it on the fire then turned back to the sink. She caught sight of Mibou out of the corner of her eye and turned round to greet him. When she saw the bruised lump and the long gash she gave a sharp intake of breath and pointed to his face.

— What happened?

He told her. She made sympathetic noises then went closer to him and peered up at his face.

— Sit down and let me have a good look.

Mibou went over to the dining nook in the corner of the kitchen and sat on the padded seat. He turned his face up and she peered at it from different angles.

— I think we should put something on that cut. Otherwise it might get infected. Have you put anything on it?

Mibou shook his head. Antoinette went over to the pantry

cupboard and pulled down the medical box. She fished around in it and found an old tube of antiseptic cream.

— I think there's still something in here. She unscrewed the top and tested it, then put the top back on and held it out to him. Do you want to do it yourself?

— No. You do it.

Antoinette put a bit of cream on her finger and Mibou flinched and closed his eyes as she spread it evenly over the cut. Then she stood back and surveyed it, as if it was a work of art.

— That's better. What about covering it?

— Whatever you think.

She found some gauze bandage, folded it and put it over the cream and most of the cut, then taped it on with some adhesive tape.

— It's not very neat.

Mibou used his finger to press the plaster more firmly on to his face.

— Better?

She nodded.

— Thanks Antoinette. Feels good.

The kettle started to whistle.

— Coffee?

— Please.

Mibou went out to the concrete patio. It was shaded by the house and despite the humidity it was still quite pleasant to be outside. He sat down at the faded bamboo table and noticed the way the lacquer had worn off and the ugly marks made by coffee cups and beer bottles. Nothing felt right. His face was still sore and there was a horrible knot of anxiety crawling around in his stomach. What he needed to do was get out his guitar and play for a couple of hours. That usually took his mind off things. He looked at his watch. It was just after nine – still plenty of time to have some breakfast and do a couple of hours of practice before his first lesson.

There was plenty to worry about. He felt like talking to
Françoise and he had to admit to himself that he missed her
a lot, much as he pretended to be happy. Could he ring her?
She was in Geneva now, still working with UNICEF. Then he
realised he'd left his phone in the kitchen. Anyway, she'd be at
work. And he was trying to stop ringing her only when he had
a problem. And when he thought about it, the last thing he
should do was to talk about Louis over the phone.

Antoinette came out with a plate of fried plantain and chili
and a cup of sweet black coffee. She put them on the table
then took Mibou off-guard by asking about Françoise.

— How's madame?

— Hey Antionette! Mibou laughed despite his bad mood.
Fine when I last spoke to her.

— When's she coming back?

— For a holiday?

—To live. She thought for a minute. Or a holiday.

— I'm not sure Antoinette. But I wish she was here now.
That was something he hadn't thought for a while; he really
was having a bad day.

Antoinette nodded as if to say 'that's more like it' then
went back into the kitchen.

Mibou thought he might be able to persuade Françoise
to come over for a holiday at least. Then he thought about
the dirty torn papers for the bar in the cardboard box. What
did that mean? Was the bar itself at risk now? If it was, he'd
really have to let her know. At least he was still alive – not
like Louis.

Suddenly he felt choked with anger. It burnt at his throat
and flooded his head. Why Louis? He felt powerless and
trapped. What could they do really? They should have just let
it go. But it might be too late for that, unless all these things
happening were just a warning. And why was he the target?
Not that he wanted anything to happen to them, but Marius

and Takashi were involved in this just as much – or more. And Mimi for that matter.

Well he couldn't change things now. Getting frustrated with himself wasn't going to help. What he needed to do was to work out who might be after him. Think about it. If he'd rattled the cage of someone on Saturday night, who might that person be? If he could work that out then he'd be able to help Marius and Takashi instead of just making trouble for himself and everyone. Could Bruno have been there? Bruno put the snake in his storeroom. Why? To get at him certainly. But knowing Bruno he could easily be doing a favour for someone. That's how he made a living, doing favours, getting people's confidence and then scamming them. And Bruno would be only too happy to help anyone who wanted to put Mibou out of business. Or worse.

Mibou thought back to last Saturday night. Most of the time at Silvers he remembered. He and Alex had played that guitar solo from Hotel California. There was a riff that was stuck in his mind and he laughed to himself when he thought about the guerre des guitars. He could sort of remember dancing with the English woman, Pamela. He'd met her for dinner at Maxime's on Sunday night and she'd reminded him about what he'd been doing and laughed about his dancing. He'd been relieved when he got her text because he thought it meant that he hadn't made too much of a fool of himself. Some hope!

Of Sunrise he couldn't remember much at all. Alex was there and they'd eaten spaghetti. He'd made a toast to Louis but that seemed harmless enough – everyone liked Louis. Though not whoever killed him of course. What about the table? Who was there? Nothing came back except Alex. Alex! Why hadn't he thought of that before? Alex would probably know. All he had to do was ring.

His mobile was in the kitchen so he took his empty plate

inside and picked up the phone from the table. Maybe it was time for a beer – that might help his memory. He took a bottle out of the fridge and a glass from the freezer and went back outside.

He scrolled through the list of contacts on his phone and found Alex's number, then he checked his credit. There wasn't much but it should be enough for a few minutes. The battery would probably run out by then anyway. He thought of texting but it seemed too complicated. The phone only rang a couple of times before Alex answered.

— Hey Mibou. What's up?

— Not much. I want to ask you something. It might sound a bit strange but one day I'll explain it to you.

— Go on.

— You know when you were over here last weekend?

— Sure. We had the big play off at Silvers. Alex laughed. Who do you think won?

— Me of course! Mibou laughed too. Most fun I've had for ages. After that we went to Sunrise. I can't tell you why right now but I really need to know who was there that night.

— At Silvers? Or just at Sunrise?

— At Sunrise.

— You've forgotten?

— Just about everything except I remember you were there.

— Yeah. You were pretty far gone that night. Let's see. There were les Lionels – they were sitting next to me. Then the rasta at the end. You were at the other end. I was on one side and that loser who calls himself a bass player was on the other side.

— The bad bassist?

— Yeah. AJ. You were talking to him most of the time. I seem to remember he was giving you a lift home. Amazing – you're always so rude to him.

— Trumped up little jerk. And what about at the other tables?

— I didn't take much notice but they seemed like the usual crowd.

There didn't seem to be anything odd about any of that. Then Mibou had a thought.

— Do you remember Bruno?

— That sleaze you used to hang out with? Once seen never forgotten. I couldn't understand what you saw in him.

Mibou wondered too.

— That's the one. Was he at Sunrise by any chance?

— No. Definitely not. I would have noticed if he was. He always gave me a bad feeling. He and his mate AJ. They both give me the creeps.

Warning beeps sounded on Mibou's phone. The battery was about to go. He was thanking Alex as the phone cut out.

Mibou would have liked to ask Alex more but it would be a few hours before his phone was recharged. He thought about AJ. So he'd been talking to him at Sunrise. He really must have been drunk. Years ago AJ had approached him after a gig one night. Mibou was always happy to work with younger musicians, so they'd met up a few times. But AJ and he had never got along and as far as Mibou could see, his playing didn't change one little bit. That's when Mibou had started calling him the bad bassist. Le mauvais bassist. It wasn't just his playing. Mibou himself had a gift – he realised that and didn't expect the same from everyone. But having a talent was only the start and he respected any musician who put in long hours of practice. Which AJ never did, yet he was so pleased with the little he could do.

And there was something else. Mibou never trusted him. AJ always had petty gossip that he wanted to pass on, usually to make trouble for people. He'd talk big about names he'd played with but Mibou quickly found out it was all talk. When he'd given AJ a chance to play with his band a couple of times, his playing was appalling. The other musicians covered for him but he never noticed, never said thanks to them. A year or so after that they'd run into each other at some gig or other and AJ was talking about the President this and the President that. Then he turned up at another gig with a brand new Gibson Thunderbird IV. No prizes for guessing who had paid for it. Not that it made his playing any better.

Mibou went into the kitchen and plugged his phone into the charger, then he went back outside and sat down again. He tilted the glass and carefully filled it with beer, then he took a couple of sips. That felt better. He put the glass back on the table and pulled another chair close so he could put his feet on it. Then he relaxed, his hands locked behind his head, and stared up into the bright green canopy of the big old almond tree. He couldn't believe that the gardener had wanted to cut it down; it was the thing he liked most about the house.

Why those early colonials had planted almond trees he could never fathom, but there was something calming about the way the branches reached out. A more obvious choice were the palm trees that grew against the wall. He noticed the crimson red of a big bunch of palm nuts that looked as if they were almost ripe. Maybe if he asked nicely Antoinette would make some palm nut soup again this year. It made him salivate just thinking about it: thick, nutty, spicy. Lots of red palm oil floating on top.

He leaned forward to pick up his beer and thought back to what Alex had just told him. So AJ and Bruno used to hang out together. That was news to Mibou but it didn't surprise him. He thought about the silver grey car and the mysterious bumper sticker.

Then an idea literally popped into his head. He took his feet off the chair and put his glass on the table. Just when he wasn't thinking about it he might have come up with the answer. It seemed so obvious that he couldn't believe he hadn't thought of it before. He knew exactly who owned the grey car. Why he would be caught up with the murders wasn't clear but it had to be his car. He looked round for his phone to ring Marius, then realised it was charging in the kitchen.

There was a loud hammering on the gate.

Now what? It sounded unnaturally loud, as if something heavy was being used to make the noise. Like the butt of a gun, he thought and felt as if his guts were turning to water. Then the bell rang. And kept ringing. Whoever it was had put their hand on it and left it there.

Antoinette came out of the kitchen door. She was holding a wet cloth in her hand and her whole face was tense with misgiving.

— Who is it?

— Not sure. Mibou tried to joke about it. Maybe not my best friends.

If we don't answer they might go away.

Mibou pointed to the face of a man that had just appeared over the top of the gate. He looked angry and gave Mibou a sour look.

— I don't think so.

The face disappeared and the noise stopped, then a harsh voice called out in a rough French accent.

— We know you're in there. Open up.

Mibou grabbed his beer and gulped down most of it. Strange how little things seem important.

— Go back inside, he whispered to Antoinette. If anything happens to me tell Marius. And Akosua.

Then he called out 'j'arrive' and walked towards the gate.

Antoinette watched through the louvres as Mibou pulled back the heavy wooden latch that he used for security at night and opened the gate. Three men pushed their way in. There was a tall man with a gun and a heavy set short man in camouflage uniform. Another man in a brown suit seemed to be in charge and she could see him say something to Mibou though she couldn't hear what it was.

The ugly man with the spotted face grabbed Mibou's arms roughly and pulled them behind his back. Then they pushed him out of the gate, leaving it swinging open. Antoinette heard an engine start up and glimpsed the dark blue of a police van as it drove past the gate. It wasn't rational, but the first thing she did was rush out and put the latch over the gate again, as if that was going to do any good.

16

When Antoinette's call came Marius was reading through the second draft of his article on the rally. He was sitting at the kitchen table opposite his niece Edith who had come over to give him a hand; she could do with a bit of extra money and he could do with her help. She reminded him a lot of Selina at that age. So slender she might have seemed fragile except for her assertive jaw, lively eyes and general air of being totally in control. Marius had read from his handwritten first draft and Edith had typed it on to Eva's computer, then she'd printed it out and he was making a few more changes.

He'd started with a description of the critically injured woman – still in a coma, he'd been back to see how she was going – and the family. To him it seemed to strike the right balance but he worried that it might sound sentimental. What had started as a lie had become an interest and he wanted it to be as good as he could make it. Though of course it wouldn't go out under his own name. He'd decided on 'Innocent Bystander' as his by-line, but he wasn't sure about that yet either. He read out a couple of lines to Edith.

— What do you think? Don't be polite. Is it dry-eyed enough?

Edith laughed and quizzed him with her eyebrows.

— Dry-eyed?

— Not sentimental.

— Okay. No really. It's good. I can't believe that it all happened downtown in Lomé and I had no idea. She looked back at the computer then up at Marius.

— Well, maybe there's something in the description of the boys. Not sure exactly what....

Then Marius' mobile rang and he held up his hand.

— Just a minute Edith. I have to take this call. Then into the phone. Antoinette. What's up? Is it Mibou?

— They've taken him away. Her voice sounded high pitched, almost hysterical.

Marius did his best to sound reassuring. In a way, Antoinette being so upset helped him to keep calm and focused.

— It's okay Antoinette. Don't worry. Did you see who it was?

— The gendarmes. There were three of them. Monsieur told me to go inside but I could see from the kitchen window. There was a tall one with a gun and a big short man. Then this other man in a brown suit.

— Is Mibou okay? Did they beat him up again?

— No. But they handcuffed his hands behind his back and took him away in the police van.

Antoinette was starting to sound more in control, her voice getting back to normal.

— They're probably just planning to give him a fright. I'm sure we can get him back. Marius thought that sounded rather odd, as if Mibou was stolen goods or something. In a way he was. How are you? Do you want me to come round?

He imagined Antoinette on the other end of the phone. She'd been working for Mibou for years now. First with Françoise and now just for Mibou. During what must be almost ten years she didn't seem to have aged at all. She was still pretty and slight with thoughtful big eyes and an air of independence that stopped short of being tough. There was something challenging in the way she held her head to one side and looked directly at you, but she only spoke when it seemed necessary. There was a pause while she considered his offer.

— No. Don't worry about me. I feel better now I've talked to you. Do you know what's happening? Monsieur's face looked awful this morning.

Marius wished he could answer that.

— Some of it but not everything. I'm sorry to be mysterious but I can't tell you yet. What you can be sure of is that Mibou hasn't done anything wrong. Nothing at all.

He could hear the relief in her voice.

— So that means you'll be able to help him.

— Yes my dear. I'll get on to it straight away. Put the bar over the gate and ring me if you have any trouble.

— I've already done that. Goodbye Mr Marius.

She hung up and Marius did the same. He sat for a while with the phone in his hand, staring into the distance and trying to work out what to do. He didn't feel nearly as optimistic as he'd tried to sound. This was really taking things too far. The charge, whatever it was, had to be trumped up. Maybe last night they thought he wouldn't have papers and were planning to take him away then. Now they'd come back and Marius knew they could make up whatever they wanted. Especially since Mibou was a foreigner here in Togo, and a musician without connections. That's what they thought anyway. He must know someone who could help.

Edith's voice interrupted his thoughts.

— Uncle Marius.

He realised now she'd said it a couple of times before he'd heard.

— Some unexpected news. Marius could see that Edith wanted him to tell her about it but there was trouble enough already. Sorry Edith. I can't tell you any more. The less you know the better. Even this article isn't exactly following the party line! He smiled at her. They had an understanding

154

about politics and that was one reason he'd asked her to help him type up the article. She reminded him a bit of his old revolutionary self. Maybe that's why they got on so well.

Edith laughed.

— No problem. I'm used to you and your secrets. Do you want to finish this? She pointed to the laptop. I've got another couple of hours or so before I have to be at my lecture.

That gave Marius an idea.

— Sorry Edith, I'm a bit distracted. I just thought of a phone call that I need to make but it won't take long. I'd really like to get the article finished while you have the time.

He went out on to the terrace to make the call. When Edith mentioned her lecture it had reminded him of his old uni friend Emil. He had a law practice here in Lomé and when Marius got through to him he said of course he could help. There were only a couple of places where Mibou could be and he'd track him down, find out what he could, probably get him out on bail at least. Marius should wait for him to call back – it might be a while.

Marius felt a lot better. He went back inside and sat down at the table then he picked up the A4 sheets and skimmed through the opening paragraphs.

— What were you saying about the boys?

— Just this bit. She pointed to the computer screen. About five lines into the second paragraph. The sentence that starts 'The little boy was solemn, his head bent…' Those two sentences sound – I don't know – overdone or something.

Marius had another look.

— You're right.

Together they worked through the article until it was how they both wanted it. Edith printed out two copies for Marius then she closed down the computer, got up from the table and stretched her hands over her head, wriggling her fingers. Marius realised he'd been working her quite hard but it was a good feeling to have the article finished. At least on that score his conscience was clear. He must remember to give a copy to Jacques.

— Where can I drop you?

— Somewhere near the library would be good. The lecture's in C Block.

— I just have to make two quick phone calls. Why don't you meet me at the car? I'm pretty sure Jojo is cleaning it for you.

— Sure. Edith gathered up her things and let herself out the French doors into the garden.

Marius needed help. He rang Takashi then Gabriel. It was frustrating not being able to explain more over the phone but the word 'crisis' did the trick. They knew he wouldn't throw that word around lightly and it summed up pretty well how he was feeling. Lunch, one hour from now at the tilapia spot in the Rue des Bars? Yes, they could make it.

He locked the French doors from inside then let himself out the laundry door and locked that too. Jojo and Edith were leaning against the sparkling brown Toyota and even before Marius could hear them, he could tell from Jojo's gestures and Edith's reactions that she was getting a now much rehearsed and very dramatic story of the black mamba incident.

They dropped Edith at the university library and Marius was glad to have some time to think as they slowly made their way back into town. Every second car seemed to be silver grey and he peered at the bumpers, looking for something that might give him a lead. If he couldn't track down the car very soon, who knew what would happen to Mibou. And come to that, why only to Mibou?

17

As Jojo negotiated the traffic Marius thought about Mibou. Why were they after him? There were the phone calls with Lillian. But he'd spoken to Lillian himself and anyone listening in would have picked up his name. No. What was happening to Mibou almost certainly had to do with Saturday night. Mibou must have said something that set off the bizarre events. At that hour of the morning and knowing Mibou, that person was almost certain to be a local musician, or some one who hangs out with musicians, like Bruno. Or worse still Paulie.

A thought was starting to form: the person they should be looking for was a musician with a fairly new model grey car. That narrowed it down to a much smaller group and despite the news about Mibou he started to feel optimistic.

Jojo was slowing down and Marius realised they were turning off the Boulevard Circulaire. There was a car-sized patch of shade under a banana palm just before the intersection to the Rue des Bars and Jojo carefully pulled into it and stopped with the engine still running. Marius got out and closed the door then leant back in the open window.

—Thanks Jojo. See what you can find out. I'll see you at the tilapia place in an hour or so.

Jojo gave him a thumbs up in acknowledgement then did a U-turn and drove back the way they'd come. He was heading to the de Brujin house to have another chat with his cousin. What Marius was hoping was that Jojo would find out

157

something that could rule Philippe out completely. It seemed less and less likely that he had anything to do with Louis' death but it would be good to know for sure.

He walked slowly up the Rue des Bars, not even noticing the thumping music, going through all the musicians he could think of who might own a grey car. Or really any car. In Lomé it wasn't easy to make a living out of music and most of the musicians he could think of used moto-taxis and public transport.

It was only when he thought he heard his name called that he took any notice of where he was. Takashi was calling out and waving to him from a table next to the low wall that separated the tilapia spot from the street. Marius walked on a few steps to the entrance to the restaurant then joined Takashi at the table. It was shielded from the sun by thick vines growing over a trellis and picked up a bit of the afternoon breeze that was blowing off the sea. Marius sighed with relief as he sat down.

— Am I glad to see you! Did you have any trouble getting away from Chez Miki?

Takashi shrugged.

— Nothing that can't be sorted out when I get back. But tell me what's happened. You sounded really worried on the phone. What's this crisis?

— It's Mibou. Antoinette rang me an hour or so ago. Some gendarmes came and arrested him. Took him away in handcuffs in the police van. It could just be some more intimidation but I think it's a lot more serious. I don't know where he's been taken but I've asked a lawyer friend of mine to try to find out and I'm waiting for him to ring back. Marius pulled out his phone and put it on the table so there was no chance of missing the call. Do you remember my friend Gabriel? He's joining us for lunch too.

— The nice policeman?

— Yep. That's the one.

The friendly waitress had spotted Marius and came over to greet him and take their orders. They decided to wait until Gabriel came to order their fish and started with a couple of bottles of Star. Takashi waited until she left.

— Mimi told me about last night at the Spot. And about the snake. So why do all that if they were going to arrest him anyway?

I can't make sense of it yet, but there's at least one person who's very worried about what Mibou knows. The trouble is that he doesn't know what it is. He can't remember.

— That's what Mimi said. He couldn't even remember how he got home.

Marius laughed and shook his head.

— That's our Mibou. But listen. I was going over things while we were driving here. Tell me what you think of this.

Marius explained to Takashi about Sunrise and his idea that a musician had something to do with the deaths and probably owned the grey car. As he spoke he could see that his theory was all speculation, but he thought it held up pretty well. When he finished he sat back and sipped on his beer.

— What do you think?

— You're definitely on the right track. In a way it's the only explanation of these weird attacks on Mibou. And when you think about it there could easily be a connection between a musician and the RPT or the military or both. They're not all like Louis! That would explain why some ordinary civilian car is being used even though the killings themselves seem to have the stamp of the military.

— That's interesting. You're right, all the musicians here aren't like Louis and when I think about it that includes drugs as well as politics. What if there are drug connections between some musos and the military, what with the drug laws…

Takashi leaned forward and interrupted.

— Of course. Louis wouldn't think of drugs. Nor Mibou.

But in lots of ways they aren't exactly typical. If a muso is, let's say, buying drugs off someone in the RPT or the military, that's a vulnerable relationship. It could explain why a musician might get himself involved in being a driver for the shootings. As you say, the drug laws are really tough.

— That's just what I was thinking. Or it could even be something more straightforward. The RPT put on a lot of musical events and from what Mibou tells me the musicians get paid good money. I'm talking about really big money. No prizes for guessing that it's more than just the music they're being paid for. It's easy to see that such a musician could have pressures put on him. And there's a pretty fine line, really none at all, between the RPT and the military. It could of course be a hanger on like Bruno. But he doesn't have a car as far as I know and then he turned up at the Spot. Why would he do that if he knew what Mibou was on to? Marius shook his head slowly. No. I think he was doing a favour for someone. But that of course means that our musician probably knows Bruno.

Talking things over with Takashi made Marius feel a lot better and it added to his feeling that they were finally getting somewhere.

Takashi poured some beer into both their glasses then sat back and pushed his hair back off his face.

— We're getting close Marius. We've got the rally and some local muso driving his car for someone who knows how to use a semi-automatic. Someone with an RPT connection. Could be militia, could be military, or a gendarme. But that's a great way to cover your tracks. Shoot from an anonymous car so no connection with the RPT can be made if you happen to be spotted.

— And that's why Louis recognises the driver. However it happened, they leave Louis' mutilated dead body on the beach, pockets stuffed with cocaine. Then when they're driving back through Agkamé Kodjo sees them. Maybe they overreact. Maybe he recognises one of them or the car. Anyway, they shoot him. Then Mibou says something on Saturday night that makes the driver think that he knows – or is about to find out – about him. They can't go around shooting everyone. People would get too suspicious. So they try some juju. But before they could know if it was working or not, they try to arrest Mibou for running an unlicensed premise. That doesn't work. Now they have him in jail under who knows what charge.

As he was talking Marius looked up and saw Gabriel driving towards them. He'd approached the tilapia spot from the coast end of the Rue des Bars and just before he reached them he stopped and parked the car under the shade of a mango tree. He got out of the car and looked over at them. Marius gave him a wave and Gabriel locked the car and came over to join them. Thank goodness he wasn't wearing his uniform, Marius thought. Not that he would usually mind, but he didn't want to attract attention to this meeting.

He'd known Gabriel since they'd been at school in Kumasi; their fathers had worked together at the college there. From when they were little boys Marius had thought of him as the angel Gabriel. His smaller than usual mouth that turned up at the corners always seemed to be placid and smiling, like the illustration in his mother's bible. And Gabriel always had a highly developed sense of right and wrong. Much as Marius knew himself to be a principled person, he wasn't good in the same way. How Gabriel ended up as a policeman had always been a puzzle to Marius, but the fact that he was gave him some faith in the system.

Tilapia for three was ordered and some more beers. Marius smiled to himself as he watched the waitress flirting with Gabriel. He tended to have that effect on women; that innocent and slightly lost look seemed to appeal to them.

— So. What do you want me to do for you? Gabriel asked.

Marius explained about Mibou. His arrest and the events leading up to it, and their suspicions.

— All very circumstantial.

— Yes. Completely. But my immediate and major concern is to see if we can get Mibou out of whatever fix he's in. He hasn't done anything at all that he could legally be charged with and it worries me. It worries me a lot.

— You're sure about that? He hasn't broken the law?

— Marius shook his head.

— All Mibou does is play his sax and guitar, teach music and get drunk on Saturday nights.

There was a low buzzing noise and Marius picked up his phone and looked to see who was calling.

— Emil, the lawyer, he explained to the others.

It wasn't hard for Takashi and Gabriel to see that whatever Emil was saying was bad news. When he finished the call Marius just sat there looking at the phone and for a few seconds he couldn't say anything. He felt like a fool for not seeing this coming. Now that he knew, it seemed so obvious.

— Come on, fill us in. What's happened? Gabriel asked.

— Sorry. I don't know if you picked it up from what I said, but they've taken Mibou in on a murder charge. Louis' murder. Marius paused to let the news sink in. He's been taken to the Prison Civile. Apparently the officers Emil spoke to turned down his request for bail and won't allow any visits either.

Gabriel shook his head slowly and Marius guessed he knew things about the prison that he didn't want to talk about.

— Your friend Mibou's in for a rough time. That place is worse than you can imagine. A murder charge! And don't think it makes a difference that he's not guilty; they'll find plenty of 'proof'. Gabriel sketched two quotation marks in the air.

Takashi turned towards Marius and spoke directly to him.

— We don't have a choice now. None at all. Somehow we have to find the driver of that grey car and come up with some proof. I'm sure can we do it, now that we know it's a musician.

As Marius was nodding and about to agree, Gabriel broke in, sounding not so much angry as frustrated and bitter.

— You're right about that. As far as I can see, that's the only way that Mibou will ever see the outside world again. And even if you do find this evidence, what then? Maybe you don't realise just how rotten the legal system is here. This isn't a democracy where the law is separate from the courts. It's a dictatorship that holds elections and there really is nothing that they can't do. And for that matter won't do.

Gabriel paused and took a long draft of his beer. Marius and Takashi both knew exactly what he meant.

— I have the beginning of a plan, Marius said. It's too soon to explain it to you but if we can find the driver I have some ideas about what we can do next. He looked at Gabriel. And I'll need your help.

Gabriel raised his shoulders and looked rather skeptical, but he sounded calmer.

— If I can, I will. Oh, and by the way, I've found out some more about Major Tete Senyo.

— Anything good? Marius asked.

Gabriel shook his head.

— Not a thing. He's the type who gives all of us a bad name. His brother is some big shot in the RPT and he uses Senyo as his personal jailer. Because Senyo has the backing of his brother and through him the RPT and the government, everyone is too scared to stand up to him. Once someone like that gets control it turns the whole law enforcement system into the reverse of what it's meant to be.

— So you're thinking he's probably behind Mibou's arrest? Takashi asked.

Gabriel nodded.

— I'm sure of it. You'd better watch out or you'll be next.

It was just what Marius was thinking himself, but it didn't

help to have Gabriel spell it out for him and it was a relief to all of them to see the food arriving.

The smell of freshly grilled fish wafted around the table as the waitress put a plate in front of each of them. Gabriel thanked her as if she'd cooked the whole meal herself and she held the bowl of water for him as he washed his hands. By the time they were dry he had her name and the time she finished work. She left the bowl on the table for the others and went off with the empty beer bottles singing to herself. They started to eat the fish and banku and Marius gave Gabriel an amused look.

— Fast work!

Gabriel smiled.

— She seems very nice. Intelligent.

Marius nodded.

— She's working to put herself through uni.

— Trust you to know that already!

They laughed and bantered as they ate their meals. It was a good to get their minds off the problem of Mibou for a few minutes. But as they pushed aside their plates and washed their hands Marius realised Gabriel might be able to help in another way.

— Do you know if there's any way we can get a message to Mibou?

Gabriel thought for a minute then nodded slowly.

— I think I should be able to arrange that. I have a friend whose brother works as a warder in the prison. That wouldn't mean anything in itself – it's not really the warders who're in charge there. But this guy is in with the chefs du bâtiment.

Marius and Takashi looked at him blankly and he went on.

— A handful of prisoners who have the real control in the prison. With the tacit complicity of the Justice Ministry of course. He read their faces. Don't ask. It's a foul, corrupt place. Any 'justice' is totally arbitrary. Mostly they'll take money and hand out privileges but even that doesn't work with some prisoners.

Marius had heard those rumours but it sounded worse than he'd thought. He tore a piece of paper out of his notebook and wrote on it then handed it to Gabriel.

— What about this Tete Senyo? If he's the one who locked Mibou up he's not going to want messages getting to him.

— Sure. It's complicated. We'll just have to see who has the power in this one. These 'chefs' each have their own areas of control. Just make sure there's nothing in the note that could compromise anyone.

— No problems there. How much will it cost?

— It's hard to say. Maybe try CFA10000. Add a pen and then Mibou might be able to get a note out to you. But be warned – it all depends on the politics. If it wasn't for Senyo I'd feel more certain.

Marius tried all his pockets and came up with five thousand. Takashi added five more and a tiny retractable pen. Gabriel wrapped them inside the note and tucked it into the pocket on his shirt.

— Another thing. It might help to have some high level support. Mibou's a big musician – what about the Cameroon community here? Would they be prepared to help.

— Good idea. I'll work on that.

— Good luck!

Gabriel gave a wave to the waitress then took his leave.

— What did you write in the note? Takashi asked.

—'There's a cold beer waiting for you'. Marius laughed. He should know it's from me and at least he'll realise we know where he is.

Takashi was a bit surprised but he could see how hard it was to write something that didn't reveal too much.

— Yes. Sounds optimistic. Now we just have to make it happen!

18

Marius had been looking out for Jojo and now he saw his very clean Toyota coming slowly along the road. Jojo parked the car in the spot under the mango tree that Gabriel had just left then he opened the door of the car and sat there waiting for them. Marius searched in his pockets then remembered that he'd given his last CFA5000 to Gabriel.

— About the bill…

— Don't worry, I've still got plenty left, Takashi said. And by the way, if we need money to make Mibou more comfortable I can help out.

Marius was relieved. This could get expensive.

— Thanks. Thanks a lot.

Takashi settled the bill and they stepped out onto the hot sandy road and walked across to where Jojo was listening to football on the radio. Marius chatted to Jojo in Ewé while Takashi lounged against the car and listened to the football. When he'd finished talking Marius had a sudden thought and pulled the notebook and pen from his pocket again. He wrote a quick note using the side of the car for support and gave Jojo a few instructions then explained to Takashi as Jojo drove off.

— I've sent a note to Henri about Mibou, Marius explained. The owner of the Regent. I think he can contact some people with clout in the Cameroonian community. Hopefully he'll get some people together at his bar in a couple of hours and I'll meet them there. Then we can decide what to do next.

— What did Jojo find out about Philippe?

— We can finally leave him out of the picture. His car's completely clean – no stickers or marks from them, nothing under the chassis. And apparently he's having an affair with a French woman. They've been meeting at the Sankara Hotel. The cook overheard a conversation they had on the phone and to clinch it the cook's cousin saw them at the hotel on the Saturday night that Louis was killed.

— It's not easy to have a private life here. Takashi didn't say it, but Marius could tell that he didn't approve.

— No, it's not our culture at all. Anyway, I'm relieved that we can cross Philippe off the list of suspects. Not for him, but for Lillian. How would she have felt? She's got enough without that. And to be honest I'm glad that my instincts were right. I've been doubting my judgment of late.

— You can't blame yourself for what happened to Mibou.

— I should have seen it coming.

— Come on. Let's do that walk that you wanted me to do with you.

They walked towards the busier end of the street and Hiplife started pumping out of the ugly speakers. The people crowded into the little bars didn't seem to notice. Takashi watched them talking and thought they must be able to lip read; otherwise he couldn't see how they could hear each other. After walking for five minutes or so they came to the junction where the Rue des Bars met the much wider street that ran to the Boulevard Circulaire on the right and on the left to the Ghana border.

Marius stopped and pointed down the road to the right.

— That's more or less where Jacques said the people in the rally were shot. There's another road parallel to this one up the other end of the Rue des Bars but this is the one that Louis was walking down.

They stood looking around them. On their right the

167

Boulevard Circulaire was not much more than twenty metres from them. The traffic was moving slowly, bumper to bumper. Moto-taxis swarmed around the cars. Heavy palls of smoke hung in the hot moist air and over the he Hiplife they could hear car horns and the sound of traffic.

The Rue des Bars didn't exactly cross the wide street but a bit to the right, closer to the traffic on the Boulevard, there was a narrow street, more like a lane, that continued in the same direction as they'd just come from.

Takashi shaded his eyes with his hand and looked carefully at the lane then the Boulevard. A car turned off the Boulevard and accelerated past them up the road towards Ghana. Takashi waited until it passed then he walked across the road to the lane. Marius followed him.

On the right of the entrance to the lane a large fan palm grew out into the road. The big fan-shaped leaves were dull with dust and sand from the road but still graceful and surprisingly true to the name. Marius and Takashi stood in front of the palm and looked down the lane. It was narrow, but wide enough to take a car, and there were tyre marks in the compacted dirt. On one side there were a few plaster-covered houses behind an assortment of walls and fences. The other side of the lane was mostly one high wall, so high it was impossible to see what was behind it. The three strands of barbed wire stretched along the top of the wall gave it a forbidding, jail-like appearance. Probably a wealthy residence, Marius thought.

Takashi walked around the fan palm and stood in its shade, looking down at the traffic on the Boulevard. He pointed at the traffic.

If I was going to shoot into a crowd down there, this is where I'd shoot from. Drive along the lane and stop so that most of the car is behind this palm. He pointed over his shoulder at the tree. The passenger in the front – or someone

in the back or both — would be on the side of the car facing
the Boulevard and they could easily fire off a few rounds
without attracting much attention. Look how quiet this road
is, and that lane doesn't look as if it gets much use.

Marius looked up and down the wide, empty road and
behind him at the palm with its carefully styled leaves.

— Yep. You're right. I didn't even notice this lane and the
tree when I came down here last time. So if you were shooting
from there what would you do next?

Takashi looked around him then walked back around the
palm.

— There are two obvious choices. One, I could drive
further into the road, do a U-turn and head back up the lane.
Or probably what I'd prefer would be to take a right up this
big road where I could drive fast away from the Boulevard and
then disappear down one of the side streets towards Ghana.

Marius nodded agreement. He could picture the whole
thing. The people in the crowd on the Boulevard waving their
palm leaves. Louis coming down the road from Duku's place,
talking to Lillian on the phone, looking forward to a beer and
tilapia with Dommie and Ajavon. The silver grey car lurking
behind the fan palm, then the shots into the crowd. He looked
across the road at the ugly grey wall that stretched from the
Rue des Bars for a hundred metres or so up the road until it
gave way to the avenue of flame trees. Then he remembered
the tyre tracks.

— I have an idea. He pointed across the road to the wall.
Let's go over there.

They crossed the quiet street and walked up towards
Duku's place along the wall. Marius explained to Takashi what
he was looking for.

— I noticed something odd when I was coming down
here last time. It had rained the night before and there was
a huge puddle and some tyre tracks right up against the wall.

There might still be some signs of them left. Then you'll see what I'm thinking.

Marius walked close to the wall, eyes to the ground. Takashi walked behind him. Neither spoke. Bits of rubbish had collected against the wall; dirty grey plastic bags, cigarette stubs, grease-stained bits of cardboard, strips from old tyres. With the sun coming from the west the wall didn't give much shade and the trapped air was thick and hot.

About halfway along Marius stopped and crouched down. Takashi did the same and saw what Marius had been looking for. The dirty, packed sand surface was still moist and the huge puddle that Marius had noticed a week ago had gone. What remained were the tyre marks that Marius had found curiously close to the wall. He had tucked it away in his mind as an oddity. In the context in which he was looking at it now, it told a story. They stood up and Marius pointed to the tyre marks.

— Louis would have been about here when he was talking to Lillian. The car could have come along the lane, waited behind the palm, shot into the crowd then turned up this road. We know from Lillian that Louis saw someone or something he described as 'incredible' at around 5.00pm. The same time as Jacques and the others heard the shots. It all fits.

Marius stepped away from the wall and stood with his arms folded, leaning back slightly, looking down the wide sandy road to the fan palm and the traffic that was still inching along the Boulevard Circulaire.

— From here Louis would have seen everything. The car, the shooting and, as the car headed up this road, whoever was in the front of the car. And they would have seen Louis looking straight at them. He sees them coming, cuts the phone and instinctively heads for the wall. They follow him in the car. Maybe he's hit. Maybe he's shot. He could have been pinned against the wall by the car. But whatever happened he's pulled into the car and his body shows up hours later on the little harbour beach.

Takashi took out a handkerchief and wiped his hands as if that might clean his mind of the disturbing image of Louis being attacked here.

— Tyre tracks? Any help there?

Marius had no idea, but they were grasping at straws.

— It's worth checking. Jojo will know someone. He checked his watch. But before I meet him we've got time for one more beer. He pointed up the road. I'm sure my friend Duku will have something cold for us at Qui est libre?

Just saying the name cheered him up.

Takashi felt relieved and smiled. There was nothing more they could do here. He looked up to where Marius was pointing at two rows of intense crimson and green flame trees.

— Let's go.

19

Wednesday March 24 – Thursday March 25

Mibou shifted his weight from his left foot on to his right foot. Both his feet ached. The wall he was leaning against was grimed with filth; he felt it and smelled it but the cell was in almost total darkness. He heard a noise and looked up to see where it was coming from: the window on the wall opposite. It was small and high up towards the ceiling but let in just enough light for him to make out two rats scrambling out through the heavy bars.

He'd been in here for hours. Five o'clock precisely was when they were locked in for the night. Mibou had done a rough count and there were nearly eighty men in here with him. Ten times the number it was intended for, he guessed. Half of them, like him, were standing around the walls. The others were on the concrete floor sleeping. They were lying on rags of straw mats top to toe, or 'sardine style' as they called it here. He'd heard stories about the jails. Even heard about 'sardine style', but he couldn't have started to imagine that this is what it meant. Now Mibou wondered if he'd get any sleep with his head between other men's feet, even if he got a chance to lie down. Probably. After standing cramped like this for so many hours his whole body was obsessed with the need to stretch out and sleep.

In the police van Mibou hadn't been too worried. He'd wished he had his mobile with him but assumed that after a few hours someone would bail him out. That was less than twelve hours ago and already that person seemed different and very naïve. Up to now, he'd thought of some of the near misses he'd had with gendarmes and police or soldiers as some sort of game. They were after money and he tried not to give it to them. Now he would give them every cent he had to get out of here but no one would take it. He was pretty sure he could rot in here for good. When he'd asked about the charges, a lawyer, a phone call, they just laughed at him and gave him some more slaps around the face. He felt the swelling under his eye. Thank god Antoinette had fixed the bandage on so well.

He'd chatted for a while with the men standing next to him and picked up quite a lot about this hell hole. He reckoned the size of the space was only about six paces long and maybe four across. The guy on his right had been in here for two years already and still hadn't been charged with anything. On the other side a Nigerian had been accused of 'wandering' but there had never been a trial, no contact with the outside, nothing. He'd been in here four years.

Mibou didn't want to think about years or even days. He just wanted to get through the night. A few men were coughing and one of them somewhere near his feet sounded as if he was dying. Tuberculosis, he was told. That one over there, pneumonia. There was no hope for them if they needed help between five in the evening and five in the morning. The door was locked and nobody came in or answered calls. With one hand Mibou held his handkerchief over his nose. At least he still had that. And he could breathe. He'd lost the panicked feeling he had when the heavy metal door was locked from the outside and the space started to fill with all their expelled air and no place to go. The oxygen in the air got less and less and the carbon dioxide was thick in the cell and increased the humidity of the already moist air. No wonder the walls felt so disgusting.

His other hand he kept in his pocket. Curled in that hand he felt the note that Marius had somehow been able to smuggle in to him. Mibou smiled to himself. 'There's a cold beer waiting for you'. It had to be Marius – who else would write that? Trust him to find someone to get a message through. He shifted back on to his left foot and tried to concentrate. Marius had got a note to him, now he was trying to think what to write to Marius.

Beyond all the hideousness of the jail, the thing that was almost impossible to bear was that he knew who owned the grey car but there seemed to be no way of getting word to the others. Much too risky to put even the initials in writing. He had no idea who he could trust and it was better not to trust anyone, he reminded himself. That was always his problem – he trusted too many people.

The sick man at his feet went into another coughing fit and Mibou pressed his handkerchief tighter over his nose. He didn't want to catch tuberculosis. Or pneumonia. The thick moist air in the cell was perfect for growing bacteria. On the floor the men squashed together moved around, disturbed by the coughing but too exhausted to do anything but sleep. In a few hours the others like Mibou who were standing should get a chance to change places. That is if they had some arrangement. Mibou didn't. He could see himself standing all night.

At least people knew he was in here, though even that didn't always help. He'd already heard terrible stories from some of the men, about how people on the outside had tried to have false charges against them dropped but with no success. That was too depressing – no point thinking about it.

He went over what Alex had said on the phone. Why hadn't he thought to ring him before? There was a thought. If Marius were to ring Alex maybe he'd make the connection. Alex was safely in Benin and Marius sort of knew him and could easily get his number. Even if the message got into the wrong hands it wouldn't put Alex at risk. Mibou felt better now he had a plan. Ring Alex. That much he could say. He wanted to put 'send money' as well. It hadn't taken long to realise that the most basic things depended on money changing hands, even something like getting clean water to wash in.

They'd probably think about the money anyway. In spite of everything he was feeling tired and he shuffled himself around so he was sideways to the wall. He put his hand up and tried resting his head against it. The wall felt clammy and greasy but his eyes closed and he went into a sort of doze for a few minutes.

Somehow the night passed. He'd been on his feet the whole time. Others swapped and got to lie down but he was starting to learn there was a system for everything – exchanges of favours, money, whatever. It wasn't even light when they'd been roughly woken, and just as they'd been locked in through the night they were locked out in the day. That wasn't so bad. It was a shock when he realised that the one meal they'd been given yesterday was the only meal they got each day. That meal was still five hours away.

In the exercise yard Mibou had found a place as far away from the stink of the latrines as possible, but a foul stench still hung in the air. He wondered if he would get used to it eventually. For a while he'd chatted to some of his cellmates and found out more than he wanted to know about the Prison Civile. They'd drifted away to kick a football around the dusty exercise yard and he sat in the dirt with his back against the grey concrete blocks, half asleep but conscious of the noises around him.

He had no idea how long he'd been sitting like that when he sensed a disturbance in the air, a change in the movements around him, that made him open his eyes. He looked up at a tall, well-built man wearing a gendarme's camouflage uniform. An iron knot twisted in his stomach. The wardens were too afraid of the men to come into this area but this man looked afraid of nothing. Groggy with sleep and stiff from sitting against the wall, it took Mibou a few seconds to push himself on to his feet. Even when he did, the gendarme made him feel small and powerless. There was something menacing about his face, even though he looked relaxed, as if he was enjoying himself. A cat playing with a mouse.

When the man finally spoke, his voice was soft and neutral. That did nothing to make Mibou feel any better.

— The great musician. He spoke in educated French, enunciating each word separately and leaving a space between them as if weighing up the truth of them as he spoke.

Mibou couldn't think of anything to say so he stayed silent. Bizarrely the lyrics of a song he'd been playing with Mimi the night before kept repeating in his head – No one to talk to, no place to go…I'm happy on the shelf….ain't misbehaving… The silence stretched to what seemed like minutes and Mibou felt like a fly trapped under a glass. The man came to a decision. He crossed his arms and Mibou could see him feeling his own muscles through the light cotton shirt.

— Major Tete Senyo, he said. You might have heard of me. He tipped his head just slightly to one side and looked at Mibou as the plantation owners must have done when deciding whether or not to buy a slave. Then he tossed his head back a fraction and his mouth made a smiling action, although his eyes just kept staring at Mibou. Again he sounded as if he was testing out the idea behind the words. Mibouré a Bidas, he went on, drug addict and murderer of Parfait Badarou. Motive jealousy.

The major raised his left eyebrow. It was the only thing that moved on his face but Mibou felt that he fell far short of what this man was expecting of such a murderer and drug addict. He also knew with a visceral certainty that a murderer and drug addict was a new identity that he wasn't going to shrug off easily. Mibou started to speak but words didn't come out and he cleared his throat and tried again.

— A mistake. I'm not a murderer. I don't take drugs. Even to himself it sounded lame.

Tete Senyo showed no expression at all. He held out his right hand, palm up.

— Give me the note.

Mibou's throat went dry and he felt as if his guts were spilling out.

— What note?

The major rolled his eyes upwards and almost allowed himself to sigh.

— The note the guard passed to you yesterday in the refectory.

Mibou thought about the note. There was nothing to incriminate Marius. This major had quite obviously found out exactly what had passed between him and the guard. He reached into his right trouser pocket, pulled out the note and put it in the major's hand and watched as he tucked it in his top pocket without a glance. So, Mibou thought, the Major already knew what was on the note. At least that wouldn't tell him anything.

Tete Senyo held out his hand again.

— And the pen.

Mibou bit his lip hard to stop tears coming to his eyes. The last link with the outside was lost. He waited until he had control again but his voice was no more than a low growl.

— What pen?

The major just snapped his fingers and looked at Mibou. It was a bored, half-amused look that made it clearer than any beating or shouting would: this man was in control.

Mibou pulled the pen out of his pocket and put it in the major's hand. This should be a dream or a nightmare. Not something that was happening to him in this squalid bare yard.

There was something almost hypnotic about the major's way of looking at him. Over his shoulder Mibou could see that the men in the exercise yard had stopped kicking the ball around and had grouped together right up the other end, as far away as they could get, as if he was toxic.

Major Senyo put the pen in his shirt pocket along with the note and gave them a satisfied pat, then he took a step closer to Mibou so that he was uncomfortably close.

— Your people thought they could interfere with my business but they know better now.

— What do you mean?

— Cameroonian this and that. Delegation. The major shook his head. Even the Cameroonian President wouldn't be able to help you. His mouth settled back into the self-satisfied smirk that was as close as he came to smiling. They were so worried about their grand musician.

So they'd been here. If the major was expecting Mibou to crumple completely at this news, it had the opposite effect. His friends, his community, they were all doing their best. They believed he was a grand musician. That was more than anyone would ever think about this sadistic jerk. Mibou took a deep breath and felt stronger and taller. He wasn't alone. Just locked up. And he wouldn't give this creep of a major the satisfaction of seeing how shocked he was.

— We'll see.

Tete Senyo just looked at him as if he were an annoying insect. The self-satisfied smirk was still there.

— And don't even think about sending a message. I've had a word to the chef.

Mibou knew who he meant. The thug that controlled this miserable lot of prisoners. He was in the block known as le fond. They seemed to be mostly from outside Togo, West African by and large but there was even a French man in with them.

The major turned abruptly and sauntered across the bare yard and out through the door to the cells.

Mibou sat back down and the other men started kicking the dirty flat ball around. Half an hour ago he'd been trying to take his mind off how hungry he was. Now he just felt sick. If he ever got out of here he promised himself that he would never get plastered again.

20

Thursday March 25

Marius was having a morning beer at the Regent, a restaurant run by Henri, a Cameroonian friend of Mibou's. He hadn't been there long – his beer was still cold – and if it hadn't been for the ghastly situation that Mibou was in he would have enjoyed sitting in the shade of the covered annex, surrounded by pots of sweet smelling gardenias, in the company of three formidable Cameroonian women. Earlier that morning they'd gone to the Prison Civile and done their best to intercede on behalf of Mibou. Now they'd come back to the Regent with only bad news to report.

The women were shocked at the way they were received; for them with all their connections and privileges, a first. They'd been left sitting on the dirty wooden benches in the reception area at the jail for more than two hours. Other people came and went handing over pots and baskets and containers filled with food and who knew what else. But no one would take their carefully prepared fish and fufu and njama-njama. After waiting all that time they'd been shown into a cluttered, dirty office and ordered to sit on torn chairs with sick looking yellow foam oozing out of the holes. A man was sitting behind the desk reading the newspaper. Even when they were there. So rude. No chance to say any of the things they'd carefully planned. When he put the paper down and looked at them it was as if they were scum. He'd asked them

180

why they bothered with a murderer like Mibouré a Bidas. He was filth. A Grade A prisoner. No food. No bail. No lawyer. No visitors. That was that.

Marius listened to the retelling several times. Though he wasn't really listening. He was thinking that there wasn't much that stood between where Mibou was now and where he could find himself if he made the slightest wrong move.

How could he have allowed himself to be so optimistic yesterday? Now he felt uncomfortable thinking back to the message he'd sent to Mibou. 'There's a cold beer waiting for you'! Now it seemed insensitive and flippant. He was glad that it was only Takashi and Gabriel who had seen it.

To be honest, perhaps it was because he felt as if he'd allowed Mibou to get into such a mess that he wanted to think it could all be fixed by influence and money. Well, he could cross that one off! The ladies with their style and connections had been treated worse than your average Togolese market woman.

Five minutes ago Gabriel had called and now Marius knew that the CFA10000 had got them exactly nowhere. Of course Gabriel had been too cautious to say much on the phone but 'failed delivery of the package' was enough. When they met up again tomorrow he'd find out more. Meanwhile Marius hoped fervently that he wasn't unknowingly setting up more victims to be knocked down like skittles. At least he'd managed to hide what he was doing from Eva and the kids, so they shouldn't be in danger. Though what about the snake? What if he hadn't found it when he did?

— You okay?

Marius realised Henri was talking to him. There was nothing at all that he wanted to share with Henri; it was all too complicated and dangerous.

— Oh. Sorry. I was just thinking about Mibou, what it must be like in that jail. Then he added. You know Henri, when you think about it, Socrates was probably right when he said that justice is to be preferred before all other things. I'm usually a Diogenes man, but that thought really seems to hit the nail on the head.

Henri looked as if he didn't have a clue what Marius was saying but he nodded in a vague sort of way and turned back to the others.

Marius had no intention of sharing any of the rest of the mess with this group of Mibou's friends. All they knew was that Mibou had been arrested and charged with Louis' murder. Shocking but not unheard of, just closer to home than usual. Socrates wouldn't have fancied living in this city of injustice and random violence. But then look what the Athenians did to him, though at least he was killed humanely.

Leaning far back in the chair Marius sipped on his glass of beer and looked up at the hazy blue sky. It helped him to focus on his thoughts. Now more than ever he had to keep his mind sharp. That evening at Chez Miki when they'd all agreed to find Louis' real killer seemed a long time ago. When was it? It was Thursday today, so go back a week to last Thursday and then back to the Sunday before that. A week and a half ago. At the time he knew more than the others – except for Takashi – the risk they were taking. But then there had been a choice. If things got too messy or dangerous they could give up. Stop their inquiries. Accept that they would never know what really happened to Louis.

Now that choice was gone. Louis had already been killed; they couldn't bring him back. But Mibou had little chance of staying alive and no chance of being free again unless they could finish what they'd started. Right now that meant finding the man with the silver grey car. And that was only the start. Then they'd have to show evidence, get someone to listen to them. And hardest of all, get that person to act.

The whole front part of Marius' head was getting tighter

and tighter and he could feel an incipient dull feeling, prelude to a headache. That wouldn't help anyone. He rubbed his temples with his fingers and breathed deeply and slowly, then he let his head relax forward. That was better. In a few quick mouthfuls he finished off his beer and went over to the bar to get another one. How much longer was Lucien going to be? The clock behind the bar said 1205. Already! Marius realised how much he was counting on Lucien to help find this car-driving musician.

Takashi had thought it would be easy enough to find that person and Marius had agreed. That seemed very naïve now. Lomé was full of musicians of one sort or another. The jazz players, the ones who played in the clubs around town – they were easy enough to find, but last night Lucien had drawn a blank on those. Marius was realising that outside his pretty wide circle of connections and friends a lot went on about which he had no clue. No clue at all.

He sat up at the bar and despite everything relished the first few mouthfuls of the very cold Gulder beer in the frosted white glass. A light afternoon breeze had started to blow in from the Atlantic and there was a faint smell of salt in the air. Much better.

The others were heading off and he waved to them. They weren't going to give up and he was glad of that. Look at Fela Kuti in Nigeria. Two years or something like that he'd been in jail but all that petitioning worked in the end and he'd been released. But then there was Ken Saro-Wiwa. Not all the petitions from the world's big shots made any difference. They killed him anyway. There was that other singer as well. Was that in Cameroon? Or Benin? What was his name? Marius gave up.

At least they'd been lucky that no one had seen him and Mimi this morning. The thought of Mimi made him smile and he let it sit there for a while. When Takashi had suggested taking the tyre prints over a beer at Duku's they'd both been in buoyant mood. The whole ambience of Duku's little Qui est libre? shop was soothing. Quiet in the afternoon, the light seemed to reflect off the green and vermillion of the tree making a cocoon of dappled shade. Marius had been reluctant at first. What about security? What if someone saw them? But Takashi had found an answer to all his objections and suggested that Mimi should help.

Mimi had to get it done before school so they'd met at 7.00am just along from the Rue des bars where the marks of a tyre were still there right next to the wall. She must have been up for hours before that getting everything ready and travelling into town, but she looked lively as ever, teasing him about how grumpy and slow he was. It was true.

She took charge and he had let her get on with it. Whatever site she'd found on the internet was pretty good. First she'd used her Pentax to photograph the marks. She'd even brought a ruler to put alongside it and took the shot again. "So we can know the size when I enlarge it," she'd said. Marius wasn't sure he would have thought of that. At least he'd been able to get his hands on some plaster of Paris that Dzigi had been using to make little models of dinosaurs.

But the hairspray was Mimi's idea. She'd pulled it out of her giant black bag with the ridiculous pink bow that somehow looked like a kitten, and for a confused minute Marius thought she was planning to do her hair. But it was to harden the surface over the marks in the sand before they put the plaster on. They'd practised on another piece of earth before they worked out the best way to do it and when he'd removed the dried plaster he was impressed how well it had worked. Jojo had been left keeping guard while it dried but according to him no one took much notice. He wondered whether it would be any help in the end, but something was better than nothing.

Mimi must have finished developing the photos by now – that is if her plan to use the dark room at school was working out. Maybe when he saw those photos he'd have a better idea how the plaster model might help. He'd certainly been surprised at the amount of detail that had shown up and Mimi seemed pretty sure that an expert could tell all sorts of things from the worn out bits and other things. Marius didn't think Jojo's experts would be up to that but you never knew. There were some very smart people in some humble positions.

When Henri opened the gate to take the women out to their car Marius caught a glimpse of Lucien's blonde dreads. At last. Let's hope he's found something Marius thought. Lucien swung himself through the gate and used one of his sticks to close it after him. As he made his way along the gravel path to the annex, Marius' phone rang. He checked the screen. Mimi. Good. He waved to Lucien and pressed the receive button.

— Ciao Mimi.

— Ciao Marius. I have the photos. Can we meet somewhere at lunchtime? She sounded excited.

— When's lunch.

— Soon. In about fifteen minutes.

— Is it too far to come to the Regent?

There was a pause while Mimi tried to remember which spot that was.

— It's the one where you sang with Mibou and Lucien on New Year's Eve.

— Henri's place? Got it. I'll be there as soon as I can. The phone went dead and Marius ended the call and put the phone back in his shirt pocket. It made him happy that he had Mimi helping him; she was like Takashi in so many ways. Marius slipped off the stool as Lucien came up and greeted him.

— What will you have?

— What you have looks good.

185

Marius ordered a bottle of Gulder and they settled themselves at the table in the annex. Lucien came straight to the point, his dry clipped voice almost a monotone in odd contrast with what he was saying.

— It's not fucking easy. I started ringing round then I thought shit. If one of these low lifes got Mibou in jail on a murder charge I might be putting my head in the same fucking noose.

Marius silently cursed himself for not warning Lucien. Make a list was all they had agreed on. To Lucien he sounded calm as ever.

— So you stopped. Who did you ring?

Lucien mentioned some names that meant nothing to Marius. He saw Marius frown and added quickly:

— Friends. They thought it was fucking crazy asking about cars. Marius gave him an appraising look from behind the beer glass he was holding in front of his face. Hey relax man. They just think I'm fucking crazy wanting to buy a car. Lucien's laugh was like his speech; clipped and flat, as if he was reading from a script that said 'ha, ha, ha'.

Sometimes the way Lucien spoke reminded Marius of Thelonius Monk, and that was how Lucien played too. Which came first: the way he spoke or the way he played? When he thought about it, Mibou spoke like he played too – big, full sound, everything out in the open.

Marius took Lucien's advice. He relaxed back in his chair and laughed.

Lucien smiled his lopsided smile and pushed a folded piece of manuscript paper across the table.

— It's a list of all the people I can remember seeing at Sunrise, he explained. If I know where they live, I've put that in too.

Marius unfolded the paper and looked at the list. At least it was a starting point.

— Good idea. I thought of talking to the fellow who owns the place but then realised I could fall into the same trap as Mibou.

— Same here.

Marius nodded and read out the first name.

— Pierre. Drums. Old market area.

Lucien shrugged.

— Best I can do.

Marius tucked the list in his pocket next to his phone.

— Thanks. It's somewhere to start looking. Any big new car is going to stand out in some of those areas you've got there. He broke off and waved to Mimi who had just come through the gate.

She came over and greeted them, then ordered herself a soda water from the bar and sat down next to Lucien.

— I've only got twenty minutes, she explained. But look at these.

On the table in front of her she wiped away the grime with a little tissue wipe, then she put a big manila envelope on the clean spot and peered inside it. She carefully picked out the photo she wanted and held it up for Marius and Lucien to see. There was no one else around and even if there was, Marius thought, looking at a photo together was a normal enough thing to do. Except this photo showed a much-enlarged print of a car tyre. Next to it were numbers and a line from the ruler.

— Look. Mimi pointed to a part of the photo that showed some small marks more or less in the shape of a square. Do you know what I think that is?

Lucien leaned closer and peered at it while Marius tried to refocus his eyes by leaning back in his chair and screwing up his eyes. Maybe he should get some glasses.

— A patch? Lucien asked.

— That's what I think. So if the car's quite new and it's

already had a puncture, whoever fixed it might remember the car. And the driver. Mimi looked at Marius, still struggling to get a clear view of the photo, and she pulled a magnifying glass out of the envelope and handed it to him. Here. Try this.

— Thanks.

With the magnifying glass it was quite remarkable what he could see.

— You're right. It looks as if there was a bolt or glass that went into the tyre. Something anyway. He looked at Lucien and Mimi. I guess it depends on where this person lives and whether he gets his car fixed there or in one of the places in town. He's a musician and despite showing off in his flash car, he's probably still living somewhere quite modest. Likely therefore to get a tyre repaired at the place down the road. In that sort of place, someone might easily remember the car. And there isn't the same problem of being recognised that there would be if we were asking questions of the musicians themselves. Definitely worth checking. Jojo and I can do that this afternoon. Marius passed the magnifying glass to Lucien.

— What do you think made that puncture? he asked Mimi.

— I couldn't work it out. That's why I kept enlarging that bit. It looks like a tear – so maybe glass?

Lucien handed her the magnifying glass and nodded.

Mimi packed the photos and the glass back into the envelope and gave them to Marius. Then she drank the last of her soda water and stood up to leave. She hesitated and looked at Marius. All the worry that she'd been trying not to show was in her face.

— What chance do you really think we have Marius? What are the chances for Mibou?

— If we can just get our hands on this musician and his car I have a little plan that might work. And we'll find him. We will find him soon.

Mimi bent over and gave him a quick kiss on both cheeks.

— Thanks. I can't stop thinking about what it must be like for him in there. That makes me feel better. And if there's anything else I can do…

Lucien took her hand as she was passing him and gave it a squeeze.

— Mibou's tougher than he seems Mimi. He'll be fine.

Mimi didn't feel convinced but she smiled her thanks. Suddenly she felt too emotional to risk trying to say anything. As she was walking along the path to the gate Mibou called out to her.

— Mimi. Before you go. I think we should all meet up tonight – the four of us. What do you think about Chez Miki? Has Takashi got students?

— No. He'll be fine with that. He was saying the same thing this morning. What time?

Marius looked at Lucien.

— Seven o'clock okay with you?

— Sure. Pick me up?

Mimi made a mental note that they'd probably be at Chez Miki's at 8.00pm and let herself out the gate to grab a moto-taxi and rush back to school.

It had been a long day and by the time darkness fell Marius was pretty sure he'd been up and down every street in Lomé. Jojo had done all the driving and Marius had plenty of time to think. Too much maybe. Place after place turned out to be a deadend. He still felt sure they would find the silver car – he couldn't even think about the alternative. Just maybe not today.

After Lucien and Mimi had left him at the Regent he'd ordered some food and looked over Lucien's list while he ate. If the musician they were looking for was in with the RPT – and Mimi's diagram made that very clear – then chances were that he came from the Kabyé people. With a pen he'd put an asterix next to the names on the list that he figured could be Kabyé. Not many. Most of the names sounded more Ewé or Mina or foreign. Not that it was foolproof – all sorts of people chose to support the RPT – but it was a starting point.

He was familiar with most of the places Lucien had jotted down. Sometimes it was just the name of a drinking spot, but Lomé was like that; some small scruffy-looking place could become a well-known bar. And no one talked in terms of streets – it was always a school, a church, a market. When Jojo had arrived to pick him up they'd made a rough plan that covered the main tyre servicing places and they made a note of musicians in that area. Then they'd set off.

That had been five hours ago. He wondered if there was a tyre servicer or motor repairer that he didn't know about. He'd made up a story about a stolen car and tried it out on the first tyre place. That didn't work; he didn't know nearly enough about the car that was supposed to be stolen from him. New, silver grey. Pathetic really. Jojo had helped and the car became an Audi A4 1.8 turbo Quattro sedan. For all they knew it might really be the make of the car they were looking for. Jojo seemed certain it was very popular in Lomé. That worked like a charm. No, not an A4 but an A6 2.8. Not sure about the model but an Audi all right. A silver grey Kia but no Audi. And on and on.

Marius was surprised by how many silver grey cars had had punctures fixed over the last year. The best lead was one in Tokoin, where one of the workers could remember pulling a shard of broken beer bottle out of a tyre. No idea if it was an Audi but newish, silver grey. Owner looked shifty – could have been a car thief. He'd follow that up tomorrow but it was time to get home and have dinner with the family before heading out to Chez Miki.

21

Thursday 25 March

For Mimi Thursday afternoon was no better than the morning. She'd spent more than one free period developing the photos and had to get everything else done super fast to make up the time. Meeting Marius at lunchtime had been rushed as well – she hadn't even had time to eat anything except some ghastly sweet biscuits from the staff room. And there was so much preparation and marking, never mind the teaching. The weekly staff meeting was always after school on Thursdays and today it had dragged on and on. She wondered why people kept asking irrelevant questions. Didn't they realise they were taking up everyone's time? When the meeting was finished Sarah suggested a drink at the Tropicana Club with Jenny, and Mimi was well and truly ready for a cold glass of white wine.

They'd ordered a big serving of French fries to share and gossiped about school things. Then Sarah announced that she refused to say one more word about school, and there was a bit of a silence while they all tried to think of something to say.

— Hey Mimi. Jenny said into the silence. I saw your boyfriend dancing with someone on Saturday night.

Mimi had no idea who Jenny was talking about so Jenny kept going.

— You know. The sax player. Your teacher. He was really hot on Saturday night.

Mimi didn't like the way Jenny always referred to Mibou as her boyfriend. She guessed it was meant to be a joke and tried to smile, but she felt a lot more like crying. If only they knew where Mibou was now!

— What do you mean hot?

— You should have seen him. He was playing the guitar like nothing else. There was some other guy as well. It was as if they were competing with each other. I've never heard anything like it before. It was amazing.

Saturday night, Mimi thought, the night of Sunrise, the beginning of the end for Mibou.

— What else did he do?

— That's it. Then a sort of friend of mine – Pamela, another Brit – was dancing with him. I think they had a date on Sunday night. That was it.

Mimi was surprised at how uncomfortable that all made her feel. She supposed she felt a bit possessive about Mibou – her teacher, her father's friend – and was a bit thrown to find out that her friends at school knew more about him than she did. It just hadn't occurred to her there would be any connection at all. But who knew? Maybe the information could help them. What about Pamela? Was she at Sunrise, Mimi wondered. Could it be a lead?

— Another drink? Sarah asked.

Mimi looked at her watch and realised how late it was. If she had another drink she could meet Marius and Lucien and get a lift home with them. It was a plan.

— Yes please.

She pushed her glass over to Sarah and took out her phone to call Marius.

22

It was a quiet night at Chez Miki. The next group of drumming students wouldn't arrive until the weekend and there was nothing extra on Thursday nights: no live music, no special banquet. Takashi had given Yao the night off and the few tourists who had called in for dinner had left by eight o'clock.

Marius and the others got there half an hour later. It had been a long day for Mimi too and she was relieved to be back home at last. She left them with Takashi and went to her room to drop off her things.

Her light cotton jacket had become dank and limp. The purple shoestring top had moist dark marks and sweat had gathered under the band of her skirt. The desert people had a point with their flowing robes she thought. Perhaps she should start a new fashion. Coming here, she'd tried to ignore the heat but now she couldn't wait to get into her old denim shorts and her favourite T-shirt. But first she sat on the side of the bed and took off her sandals. They were fun – bright green with big ankle straps and chunky heels – but now she was home she realised her feet were killing her. She had a quick shower then rubbed some peppermint cream into her feet and thought about what Jenny had told her.

She'd felt terrible when Jenny talked about Mibou playing at Silvers. What if Mibou really did end up dead like Louis? Only a couple of weeks ago she'd been singing with them both. Then just after that there was the shocking news about

Louis. And now Mibou was in jail. Suddenly she'd burst into tears and couldn't stop crying; it was the first time she'd cried since she'd heard the news about Louis. She realised how much she'd been holding in, and not being able to talk about it with her friends made it worse. Jenny and Sarah had been really kind and understanding but Mimi couldn't say anything about Mibou being in jail. How would that place him with the school?

In the car coming out here she hadn't said anything to Marius and Lucien; she was worried that she'd start crying again if she tried to talk. If they noticed her silence they didn't say anything and Mimi was relieved. She must remember to tell them about Silvers later. Or maybe it was just trivial gossip. She'd wait and see how things went.

Stepping up close to the long mirror in the bedroom she was surprised to see how normal she looked. But her eyes were small from all that crying. With a fine brush she drew a black line around her eyelids, then she rubbed in some grey eye shadow and brushed some soft green powder over it. She blinked a few times and looked again. Better.

Feeling recovered she joined the others. As usual they were lounging in the padded bamboo couches next to the garden. The breeze that blew from the sea in the afternoon had dropped and the noise of the cicadas sounded loud in the stillness. Smoke from the new citrus burners drifted up slowly and scented the dark air. Mimi approved of Takashi's campaign to keep the mosquitos away and thought the lemon smell was much better than those ghastly Tiger coils.

Marius was bringing Takashi up to date with the day's news. He'd brought along the photos that Mimi had developed and Takashi was holding them up to the light that hung down from the beams over the low table. As Mimi came and sat on the couch next to him he put them back on the table and looked at them through the magnifying glass.

— What do you think? She asked.

— They're very good. So clear.

Mimi leaned over and stretched up with her hand, pointing to the part where the symmetrical pattern of the tyre treads was interrupted by a small jagged line.

— What do you think this is?

Takashi put the magnifying glass closer to his eye and moved the photo in and out to get focus.

— Glass. Or a sharp stone. He pointed at the slightly uneven line that was just discernible cutting across two of the tread marks. See how it's not straight?

— Exactly.

Marius watched the smoke from the citrus burners wafting gently in front of him and tried to grab hold of a thought that was just out of reach. It was the mention of glass that set it off. It had been annoying him all afternoon. But his head was filled with more than he ever wanted to know about tyres and it felt like mush.

Takashi put the photo back in the envelope with the others.

— What about the tyre people? Could Jojo's expert help?

— The expert turned out to be a character who I strongly suspect makes his living stealing tyres and reselling them. Not your cheap Chinese brands. The ones he showed us were all Pirelli, Bridgestone, Michelin. Jojo denies it of course – that he's stealing them. Anyway he knew his stuff and seemed to think it was perfectly normal for us to have a giant photo of a tyre mark. I think he's the Robin Hood of the tyre-thief world. Steals from the rich and sells to the poor. A very enterprising fellow I thought.

Marius laughed, remembering the surprisingly smart looking chap and his 'store' set up under the trees on the side of the road. Organised and neat for that sort of thing.

Takashi wasn't sure what to think about the way the people here described someone as enterprising when they could just as easily have used the word dishonest.

— So long as he leaves my Suzuki alone.

That made them all laugh and Mimi laughed so much it took a minute before she could say anything.

— No one would steal your car, let alone your tyres. She bust out laughing again and added. People run away from your car. Even you never drive it.

It was true but Takashi pretended to be hurt and the look on his face set them off laughing again. Just thinking about Takashi's loyalty to the strange little blue car that had spent most of its life with one problem or another made them laugh.

When Marius finally stopped laughing he felt better for it, sharper; it seemed to have cleared his head.

— What I was going to say is that I have some good news. Our Robin Hood is pretty sure the car we're looking for is a BMW. Just a second. He picked up his notebook and read from it. Probably a Series 3 executive sedan. He said a lot about something to do with flat tyres.

— Flat-run tyres? Lucien asked.

— That's it. Flat-run.

— So now we know the car was a silver grey BMW something. Anything else? Takashi asked.

— There was a place out near the airport where a chap could remember taking a shard of a beer bottle out of a tyre on a silver grey car and repairing it. Wasn't always possible, he said. Last week, he thought, but it could easily be a bit longer than that. I think we might be closing in.

Today had seemed like a week and frankly he was exhausted. Looking for a needle in a haystack would have been easier, he thought. But now things were starting to fit together. Marius could feel it like an extra sense. Suddenly the thought he'd been trying to bring to mind all day popped into his head and he leaned forward towards Takashi.

— You know the place where we think the car was parked while they were shooting at the demonstrators?

— Behind the fan palm?

— Exactly. I might be making it up, but I think there was broken glass on the ground.

Takashi visualised the narrow dirty lane. It was the sort of place where there could have been broken glass but he wasn't sure and he shook his head.

— Sorry. There probably was glass there but I'm not sure. Are you thinking of where the car picked up the puncture? The glass might still be there.

— Precisely. And it could be a bit more evidence.

Takashi thought back to the feeling he'd had when they'd been standing near the fan palm. A strong sense of story was the way he put it to himself. Since that time he'd been convinced they would find the car and the driver and the killer. He didn't believe in ghosts, otherwise he might have thought someone was communicating with him. Like Louis.

— Where was this tyre place?

— Out towards the airport.

— Any chance of getting a name from the mechanic?

Marius shook his head.

— No. The owner of the car wasn't a regular.

— If it was our man, he probably didn't want people who know him asking questions.

— So we're closer but still miles away. Lucien had been listening quietly. Now his blunt statement spoken in his flat monotone was like a cold shower.

There was silence as the others acknowledged the truth of what he had said. Mimi listened to the night sounds and was suddenly conscious of drums beating in the distance. It was almost a nightly event these days. She was trying to put together what they knew now and what more they needed to know. At least the time she'd spent on developing and enlarging the photos hadn't been wasted. So they knew the make of the car. They might even know where the glass had come from.

But they didn't know who it was and finding the place where the car had been fixed wasn't giving them the answer they'd been hoping for. There was the thing Jenny had told her about Saturday night. Could that help? Anything was worth a try. The others might see something she didn't.

It was a relief to all of them when she broke into the depressed silence.

— There's something I found out today – it's about Mibou on Saturday night. I can't see how it helps but anyway….My friend Jenny was at Silvers that night and she said Mibou was playing guitar like a crazy man. He and this other guy were having a sort of battle with their guitars. Then she said he was dancing with a friend of hers. Pamela someone. A Brit. I guess it doesn't really help. To her own ears it sounded feeble and she wondered why she'd bothered telling them.

Lucien suddenly came to life. His eyes were sparkling but he still spoke in his clipped monotone.

— That would be Alex. I didn't realise he was in town that weekend. He and Mibou love to show off on their guitars. He remembered some of their famous 'battles' and laughed at the thought. Mad fuckers. But you know what this means?

No one said anything. Lucien looked at them, enjoying the suspense.

— It means Alex was almost certainly at Sunrise with Mibou on Saturday night. It's what they always do. And we don't have to worry about ringing Alex. Lives in Benin – one of Louis' best friends – no way he would fuck around with people like Bruno and Paulie. As he talked he took his phone out and started checking his contacts. Here. He held the phone out to Marius. Ring him. Marius took the phone. Where had he heard Alex mentioned? Takashi broke into his thoughts.

— Alex. Didn't Lillian say that's who Louis was going to jam with on the night he was killed?

— Yes. That was it. Marius remembered now. But Louis never made it. Good idea Lucien. Sure it's okay to use your phone?

— Why not? No one takes any notice of me. He laughed and gestured towards his deformed legs. Go on.

— Tell you what. You put the call through and explain then give the phone to me. In fact why don't you just make the call?

Lucien took the phone back and dialed Alex's number.

The phone rang. And rang. Lucien tried again.

— Answer the phone he muttered under his breath. He waited a minute, then tried again. This time a deep, heavily accented French voice on the other end of the line said 'Lucien'.

— Hey Alex. Are you in Benin?

— Yep. Came home on Monday. Had some great gigs in Accra last week. What's up?

— It's about Mibou.

— What's going on? He rang yesterday and sounded a bit weird.

— Things are pretty bad. He's in the Prison Civile. Charged with Louis' murder if you can believe it.

— You're kidding!

— Afraid not. Anyway, listen. Were you at Sunrise with Mibou last Saturday night?

— That's what Mibou asked me. I told him all about it when he rang yesterday. Where is he? What's this thing about Sunrise?

— Something might have happened there that put Mibou in jail. Any ideas? Like, who was there? Who was he talking to?

— God. Poor Mibou! I can't believe it. I'll tell you what I told him. There were les Lionels, the mad rasta and AJ and me. Plus a few people at the table next to us. No idea who. Mibou wanted to know if that shit Bruno was there but I told him he wasn't. And I told him AJ took him home – he couldn't even remember that. Listen, what's going to happen to Mibou? Can I help?

— You already have.

— Let me know how things go.

— Sure. And thanks. Thanks a lot.

He finished the call and repeated what Alex had told him.

— Who's this AJ that took Mibou home? Marius asked. Should I know him?

It was in that second that Lucien suddenly realised. He made a soft whistling sound and shook his head, hardly able to believe what had just become obvious to him.

— You know what I was going to say? I was going to say AJ is le mauvais bassist. And has a car. Le mauvais bassist. That's what Mibou always called him. And Louis and I used to call him that too.

The others looked at him blankly and then it hit Marius.

— Mauvais! It's one of the last things Louis said to Lillian. You're saying the man driving the silver car was this AJ. We thought it was the situation, or something bad that he saw. But it was a person. And a musician at that. Someone he knew.

— Yeah. Louis knew him. It must have been AJ driving that car because there's something else. He owns a Gibson Thunderbird bass. Can't play to save himself but he owns a Gibson. The wanker.

— Gi? Takashi asked. Gibson?

— Who's got some paper and a pen?

Marius produced his notebook and Lucien turned to a new page and wrote the letters Gibson. Tall, slanted and close together. The G looked a bit like a Y.

He showed it to them.

— The logo's something like this.

— So that's what Ama saw, Mimi said. The bumper sticker. It has to be.

— What do you know about him? Marius asked. Where he lives?

— Not exactly. On the west side I think – towards the Kpalimé bus station somewhere.

— We'll find it. Now we have the name. The initials anyway. Do you know what they stand for?

— Some long name. No idea what. Everyone calls him AJ.

— What about an RPT connection?

— Rumour is that he hangs out with Paulie – the President's fat brother. He thinks he's a bass player too. If you ask me, that's where AJ's car came from.

— And the Gibson?

— AJ gets paid to put on music events for the Presidential shows. You know – when there's a big shot in town. Army stuff as well. There's big money in that but it's more than money they want from you. This Paulie wanted Mibou to do some big event after he won that music award. Mibou turned it down.

— Lucien, Mimi asked, did you say that Mibou rang Alex yesterday?

— That's what he said.

— So if you worked out who the driver of the car was, then he probably did too. God! Poor Mibou. How must he feel?

But at least things were starting to fall into place in a way they could hardly believe. The feeling of relief was overwhelming; even the night air seemed lighter. Takashi stood up and stretched.

— Time for a drink, I think. So much to do still. But at least we know where to start.

It was only then Marius realised how intense they'd all been. No one had even thought of a drink.

— What a splendid idea. I'll help you.

When each of them had a drink in their hand they drank to the memory of Louis. They drank to Mibou and tried to imagine what it must be like for him. Then they drank to each other. Mimi christened Chez Miki the 5th precinct and Lucien made jokes about the special squad.

At the start of the day things had looked pretty much impossible. That had changed to possible, but Marius had no intention of underestimating what it would take to corner Louis' killers. Others might throw around the word 'miracle' and that would be nice too, but he didn't go along with that nonsense: it was going to be up to him to make it happen. Anyway, there was no point worrying about that now – tomorrow would come soon enough – so he let himself be carried along with Mimi and Lucien and relaxed for a while.

On the way home he took the cashew brandy from under the seat and sipped from the bottle every so often. Just enough to warm his insides and to help him plan the next and trickiest stage.

23

Behind the grey walls of the Prison Civile du Togo, Mibou lay sweating on a thin straw mat. To be precise, half a straw mat. He had no idea what time it was. The humid air was thick with the night breath of too many men. At some point he'd fallen asleep but now he was awake. The rat had come back. Was it the same rat? It had been sniffing around his legs and he'd shaken it off but his whole being felt assaulted. For a while he lay still and alert, waiting to see if it would come back, but eventually he saw it climb outside through the bars of the high window and he relaxed a bit.

At least he was lying down tonight, thanks to Umar – or Le Noir as the other men called the big Nigerian. Mibou had vaguely recognised him as a regular at the Mandingue jazz club and Umar of course knew him. It was over a year since Umar had been dragged out of his house in the early hours of the morning. He reckoned it was his neighbour, who was jealous of Umar's cyber cafés that took business away from his communication centres. It seemed that a body had turned up on the road in the street where his house was and the neighbour had told police that Umar had murdered him. When they searched his house they found things that didn't belong to him – like blood-soaked socks in his shoes and a bloodstained machete in the shrubs in his garden. There'd been no trial yet and no official charge.

Umar had been pretty excited to see Mibou and persuaded him to sing a few standards. Mibou laughed to himself at the irony of singing 'What a wonderful world' in the bare yard with the stench of the latrines in the air. I see trees of green, red roses too! Hardly. A bit of a crowd had gathered. Some joined in – time passed better for it. Music. That's all he had. No one ever seemed to want to pay much for it but in here it had a pretty high value. Umar was quite the entrepreneur and had looked after Mibou like an agent. Who would have thought! At least it got him half a mat on the floor for the whole night and other things too, like access to the washroom.

His back was starting to ache and he carefully rolled to his right side so that part of his backside was off the floor. He cupped his ear on his hand and tried to get comfortable, but his left hipbone was digging into the concrete floor that the mat did little to soften. Then there was the smell from the dirty shoes that were right in his face. He rolled over onto his back again and tried to sleep, but the man dying of pneumonia was heaving for air and the dry tubercular cough of another man had started up again.

Then he started thinking about AJ again and his head went tight with anger and frustration. The rotten piece of shit. It still seemed unbelievable that he would kill Louis, but it had to be him driving the car. Just had to be. Ten minutes later and he could have passed on AJ's name to Marius, but those pigs of gendarmes had come just then. If only he had kept his phone charged. There wasn't any point going over and over it. But he was going over and over it. Would the others be able to work out that it was AJ? How could he have been so stupid? Guilt and anxiety were eating at his insides. He should try to stop thinking but he couldn't. Even taking a deep breath was hard and now he was fully awake.

To take his mind off everything he started to compose a song in his head.

Nous somme les hommes qui on a oublié
Donnez-nous notre liberté
Not bad for a sort of chorus.

Comme les poissons a nuit, comme chiens pendant la jour....A tune started to form itself around the words as he sank back into a restless sleep.

24

'Sixteen paces / By twenty-three. They hold / Siege against humanity /And Truth / Employing time to drill through to his sanity.' Marius put down the book of Soyinka's poems he'd been reading and sipped on his mug of lemongrass tea. Is that how Mibou was feeling? Was he in a place sixteen paces by twenty-three? How big was that anyway – were the steps big or small? Soyinka was famously held in isolation in a tiny cell, so Marius decided they must have been tiny steps.

He'd been awake half the night but still woke early, worrying about Mibou and going over various scenarios for today. By six o'clock he abandoned the attempt to get back to sleep and came downstairs and out onto the terrace. The air was fresh, and sitting in the old cane chair watching the clouds change colour as the sun rose, he felt calmer, more optimistic.

At least Eva now knew what he was trying to do. She'd been listening to music when he'd got back from Chez Miki's and it was a chance too good to miss. Now that Mibou was in jail Marius knew it was probably only a matter of time before 'they' would be on to him. Eva had to be brought into the picture; if something happened to him and he disappeared she should at least know why.

In some ways she'd been relieved to find out what was going on – especially given the mamba incident – but just as he knew she would be, she was worried at the risk he was taking and the situation that put her and both their children in. Marius had told her his plan to enlist the help of her cousin Emmanuel and she'd agreed with him that it was probably the only way he was likely to get anywhere. They'd talked it over for hours and he had to admit that the seemingly endless questions her logical mind kept throwing at him had helped to show up the flaws in his plans. After she went to bed he'd stayed up for longer, too much on his mind to sleep. If he couldn't get Mibou out of this mess he didn't think he could live with himself.

He picked up his mug of tea and walked across the lawn to the tall totem pole. Dew was still thick on the patchy grass and it splashed on to his feet through his open sandals. From the kitchen he could hear Dzigi and Seri arguing about something. Eva was ignoring them, packing lunches and drinking coffee. Every so often she asked them a question. Did they have their homework? Their sports clothes? Usually he'd be in there helping, but things weren't usual and wouldn't be unless he could make his plan work.

He turned back to the totem. There were three figures on the pole, one on top of each other. It had always been the wise look of the man on top that had appealed to Marius, but below him there was a farmer holding a machete then under him a musician with a dondo slung over his shoulder. If he imagined AJ as the musician at the bottom with the talking drum, his passenger, the killer, would be the figure in the middle, the one with the machete. So who was on top? Finding the machete man would help, but if the man on the top turned out to be beyond the law, the plan would backfire completely onto Marius himself.

It was pretty clear that the attacks on Mibou were from different people and whatever Mibou had passed on had gone from the bottom to the top. The sort of man who could get Mibou locked up on a murder charge wasn't the same man who thought of using a black mamba and some cheap juju. It could be someone like the Justice minister, or an army general or the President himself. Or maybe one of the President's family. Marius knew something of the politics of dictatorship and hoped that it would play into his hands. First he had to find the man at the bottom and put enough pressure on him so hopefully he would bring the others down as well.

Marius walked back to the terrace, put his mug on the rickety glass table then sank back into the chair. What he had realised last night was that he was making a mistake looking for a silver car. AJ probably panicked because of what he thought Mibou knew about the car. So what would he do? Let's say he contacted Bruno and they hatched up the crazy plan with the mamba, but meanwhile what about the car? Hide it? But for how long? Sell it? Not likely. Disguise it somehow? AJ had no idea who might be watching out for his car. There weren't many ways you could disguise it; the most obvious one would be to change the colour. AJ's friends might find it strange but they weren't the ones he had to worry about.

Change the colour. Imagine he did that. Would he do it at a local place? Or somewhere else? Locally. Definitely. All his neighbours would see it anyway. Unless he were to get a proper job done with the dealer. That wasn't likely for a musician. No. Local was the best bet.

Marius finished his tea and took the empty mug back into the kitchen. He poured some more of the infusion from the saucepan through a strainer into his mug and took it back to the terrace. If he were in AJ's position, he would worry about attracting attention. Why would he want to get the colour of his lovely silver car changed? Marius tried to think himself into his old operational self. He'd create a reason for the change. Like damage done to the car, for instance. Something sharp dragged along the sides – not hard to do. Then he could just take it to some local place and get it fixed, no eyebrows raised.

The terrace door made a scraping sound on the paving stones and for a second Marius felt his heart jump, but when he looked around he saw it was only Dzigi trying to squeeze through the narrow gap. He got up and lifted the door so it opened wider. Without saying anything Dzigi just stood there in his neatly pressed yellow shirt and brown shorts, the leather satchel on his back. Marius squatted down and gave him a hug. Dzigi put his arms around Marius's neck and squeezed it tight then ran across the lawn to the car. Eva and Seri were already in the car and as soon as Dzigi climbed into the back and shut the door they headed off, Jojo driving, looking serious as usual. Today, Marius thought, there's a good reason for that.

He sat back down and forced himself to think step by step. The more he thought about it, the more he was convinced that AJ would have changed the colour of the car. After all that driving around, he had a rough idea of where AJ might get that done. Could be somewhere around the tyre place near the airport or further towards the Kpalimé bus station. A manageable area to search, but he and Jojo couldn't go back there. They'd done the rounds yesterday and a second visit would be inviting trouble.

It had to be someone a bit outside his circle but sympathetic to what he was doing. A smart sort of person who could improvise and follow a lead, but who wouldn't attract attention. Someone who could be trusted completely.

Marius went through his contacts one by one but none of them was quite right. He wasn't getting anywhere and time was ticking away. To give his mind a break he went into his study and picked up the final version of the article he'd written. He wanted to read it over one more time before he put it in the mail. What an interesting person Edith was becoming – she was definitely going to make a mark one of these days.

That was it! Marc. Marc, Edith's boyfriend. Why hadn't he thought of him before? The other day Edith had told him that

Marc was bored; finished university and waiting to hear about a postgraduate scholarship in France. Marius had met Marc a few times and liked the tall, extrovert young man with his socialist politics and a dry-eyed take on the world.

An hour later Marius and Marc were sitting at a table in the adobe courtyard of an African-Mexican restaurant just off the Avenue de la Paix, ten minutes or so from the airport. A map of Lomé took up most of the table and condensation from the green Star bottles was seeping into the edges of it. Neither of them noticed. The humidity in the air had already turned the map limp and the pen Marius was using made blurred smudges as he marked places on the map.

— This is the place where the tyre was repaired. Marius looked up and oriented himself, then pointed to the right. It's up the avenue and a couple of blocks in just before the turn off to the airport. He turned back to the map and circled a few blocks to the west. And this is roughly the area where AJ lives and where he's probably having the car repainted.

— You're guessing about that, right?

— Sure. But Jojo and I did a fair bit of asking around and it seems the right place to start looking to me.

— So what exactly do you want me to do?

— You want a repaint job done on your car and you're getting quotes. Sure your friend doesn't mind you using his car?

— Not at all. He'd probably be happy if I really got it repainted. Did you see it outside?

— That battered looking red car? Marc laughed and nodded. Even better. So you ask if you could see the sort of work they do and look around as much as you can. You're looking for a BMW. I could give you more info and tell you its life story but I'm not sure if that would help. What do you know about BMWs?

— The logo's easy to spot – for one thing it says BMW. Apart from that not much.

— The original colour's silver grey. There's a series number on the back of the car to the right of boot and it will probably be 3.18 SE but that's just a guess. Jojo's expert's guess, not mine. And we think it had a sticker that looked like this on the back bumper.

Marius pulled out his notebook and showed Lucien's drawing to Marc. The letters had started to smudge from being in his pocket but you could still make out Gibson.

— That I do recognise. Good old Gibson. Not many of those around in Lomé.

— You play?

— Used to when I was at school. Mibou's a bit of a standout for me. Saturday nights at Silvers he really goes off. I still can't believe that he's been thrown into jail. It doesn't make any sense.

— None. No pressure, but finding that car could make the difference for us.

— Don't worry. I'm pretty good at getting things out of people. Just ask Edith! Marc laughed and Marius thought he probably was. There was something engaging about him.

Marc poured the rest of the beer into his glass and drank it down in one gulp then put the glass on the table with a flourish. He pointed at the circle Marius had drawn on the map.

— This area here then. Any ideas on where to start?

Marius thought about what Lucien had said about the Kpalimé bus stop and pointed to a cross on the map.

— Start here and work back across towards the airport. If my logic is right, I think you'll find it pretty quickly.

— Right then. I'll get to work. Marc folded up the map. Carefully, Marius noticed, making sure that he used the same folds.

— And Marc. Be very careful. If you find the car, make sure No one has any idea that you're interested in it. I mean really sure. There's some pretty nasty stuff going on.

— Should I ring you?

— Sorry, I should have said. Definitely ring me – it's critical. But don't say anything about a car. Just ask to meet me for a drink somewhere.

— Okay.

Marc raised his hand in farewell. Marius listened as he started the car. There was a high-pitched whine from the fan belt and an unmuffled roar, then silence.

Marius ordered another beer and dialed the number for Gabriel.

25

Marc was feeling the heat. He was starting to see a pattern to the layout of these auto-repair places. This was his third and so far they'd been run-down establishments off dirty back streets where the heat of the sun intensified between buildings thrown together with corrugated iron.

This one had an L-shaped yard that wrapped around a roomy shed. The corrugated iron was rusted and derelict looking but it was on a solid concrete slab and the half raised roller doors across the wide front looked as if they'd been installed fairly recently. A small room – probably an office – was on one side at the back but the rest of the space was taken up with a few helpless looking half-disembowelled cars. In between were the parts that had come out of the cars and untidy piles of tools and old rags. On one side there was a black Mercedes Benz sitting awkwardly on a makeshift ramp.

But the thing that caught Marc's eye was a dark green car near the front of the yard that was to one side of the building. The rear of the car was towards him and he noticed a BMW logo and to the right 3.18 SE clearly marked out in chrome lettering. He walked around to the front and there were strips of masking tape around the edges of the windscreen, also covered in dark green. If it hadn't been for those, Marc wouldn't have realised the car was in what he now took to be the final stage of a paint job. Nice colour. He walked back around the car. From that angle the painting looked completely

213

finished but the car was missing its bumper bar. Then he saw what he was looking for in a pile of them stacked against the corrugated iron fence.

— Looking for something?

The man had come up behind him very quietly. His words sounded as much a threat as a question. He was holding a large shifter in one hand and wiping the grease off his other hand on the back of dirty khaki shorts. Marc had a strange thought that this man with his dark skin and grease-stained singlet and shorts was some animated extension of the workshop.

— Good paint job. I like the colour. The man said nothing so Marc went on. Thought I might get my car repainted. Dark grey maybe – or even that sort of dark green. He nodded towards the BMW. That's my car over there. Marc pointed to the old red Opel that he'd squeezed into a space just inside the fence that closed in the yard.

The man nodded and walked over to the Opel. Marc followed. He didn't feel comfortable. At the other repair shops the men had been friendly, teasing him about the old Opel, throwing in a few clichéd jokes. He shrugged off the feeling. Just a different type – not everyone had to be upbeat.

The man was running his hands over the dents and scratches on the Opel. One side had long streaks of white paint from a parking incident.

— Could do with a paint job.

— How much do you think it would be?

— Come inside. The boss'll give you a quote.

— Roughly? Marc just wanted to get away and ring Marius.

— Depends what you want done.

— Not too much. Just enough to impress the girls. That had got a laugh at the other places. This time it was only Marc laughing.

— Like I say the boss does the quotes. This way. Come into the office.

Marius had said to be careful and it would look odd if he backed out now. Marc followed the man between the cars and clutter to the small windowless room at the back of the workshop.

There was a jumble of faded yellow account books strewn over a table. A couple of battered metal cabinets looked as if they might collapse under piles of broken, discarded tools, car parts, cans of spray paint and who knew what else. On the wall behind the desk was a very faded, framed picture of Gnassingbé Eyédama.

At first Marc felt reassured by the well-dressed man who greeted him at the door to the office.

— Come in, have a seat.

Marc was happy enough to sit down. At least it was a bit cooler in here.

Then he heard the door close and the sound of a key turning in the lock.

215

26

As soon as he'd finished talking to Gabriel, Marius had taken a moto-taxi out to Klikamé and now he was sitting back in an armchair listening to his friend Bella.

— Abéyobjoli Jouriass. That's his full name. Such a shame you know. He was really quite a nice little boy when I knew his family, but no one trusts him now. No one.

Bella came over and put a glass of wine on a crocheted white doily that covered most of a small table next to Marius. He nodded and watched her pick up another one from the nest of tables and put it alongside the chair opposite him. Then she took the other glass of wine off the tray on the coffee table and sat down with a sigh.

— It's good to see you Marius. You haven't changed a bit.

Marius laughed and took a sip of his wine.

— I was an old man at twenty! There are some advantages. It's good to see you too Bella.

— I've filled out a bit. Look at me. Bella laughed and held her arms out in invitation. She was wearing a bright kaftan and matching headscarf tied high with an elaborate twist. Her round face with the dark-lashed big eyes had indeed filled out a bit since Marius last saw her, and she looked splendid.

— It suits you. Marius meant it. Why hadn't he thought of Bella before? Their friendship went back to the days when he and Selina were going out and Bella was an aspiring singer and

216

friend of Selina's cousin George. Everyone had thought she'd marry George, but Bella's career suddenly took off and she'd left for France. Now she went back and forth between Togo and France, recording and giving concerts.

— So, AJ's in trouble?

— Looks like it. If I'm right. I'm sorry I can't tell you more but it's serious. What else can you tell me about him?

Bella thought for a minute before she replied.

— Well, he's a lousy musician! But it's more than that. He acts as if he's better than everyone else but at the same time he sees himself as a victim, so he's always blaming things on other people. Like, when he couldn't get a riff, or a rhythm, he'd accuse one of the other players, or blame his bass, or whatever.

— Can you tell me what he looks like?

— It's been a while since I saw him, but he's short and stocky – you might even say a bit fat. Has an arrogant look as if there's a peg on his nose.

Marius laughed.

— Shouldn't be too hard to miss! You wouldn't happen to have his address would you?

— Probably. All sorts of musicians give me their cards. Always hoping they might get a gig with me – and the good ones do. I keep them all.

Bella pulled herself up from the armchair and went over to a drawer in the elaborately carved sideboard. She took out a box and put it on the table next to Marius.

— Here, have a look.

It didn't take Marius long. The box of index cards was neatly divided according to the alphabet; Bella had always been very organised. It wasn't just her voice and songwriting that had got her to where she was.

— Can I borrow this? Marius asked, holding up one of the cards.

— Keep it. I'm never going to use it.

Marius finished his wine and stood up ready to leave.

— I'm really sorry I can't stay and have a chat but let's meet up again before too long.

— Love to. I'll be in town for another few months. Then you can tell me what this is all about.

— It's a promise. And wish me luck.

Bella raised her eyebrows but said nothing and went over and gave him a hug.

— Good luck. Look after yourself. By the way, I was so sorry to hear about Selina. I miss those old days.

— Me too. More than you can imagine!

As the security guard opened the gate Marius turned and looked back up the drive. Bella was still standing on the verandah watching him. He gave her a wave then headed right along the sandy lane. Still the same Bella.

What a stroke of luck that she'd had AJ's name and address. Well, probably not luck. Marius kicked himself that he hadn't thought of her yesterday, but there was nothing he could do about it now. What he had to do was act fast and keep one step ahead. That much was clear.

He took his phone out of his pocket and called Jojo as he walked along. He was tempted to take the risk and give Jojo instructions over the phone but thought better of it, and organised to meet him at the Grande École crossroads. Marius checked the time: 11.50 already. That would just give him time to meet with Jojo, look for glass from the broken bottle at Rue Ibis, and then get to Joie de boire by 12.30 and meet Gabriel. At least Bella's place wasn't too far out of town.

He'd only walked for five minutes or so when he came to the main road. Great. Moto-taxis galore. He flagged the first one that came along and settled himself on the seat behind the driver. The traffic fumes and dust were bad on this main road and he was relieved when the driver decided to take the back streets.

No word from Marc yet. Marius checked the time then realised that he'd only just done that. He had to keep calm and stop worrying. Marc was resourceful and smart. Of course he'd be fine. It would be nice to get that phone call though and Marius realised how anxious he was. But to be honest he was excited as well, with that sort of tautness he felt when he was about to checkmate his Russian friend Boris at the end of a chess game.

Jojo was waiting at the crossroads, sitting in the car under the shade of a mango tree. Marius told the moto-taxi driver to wait and took only a minute to pass the card with the address to Jojo.

He pointed to the street name and explained.

— This is where AJ lives. It's the long street that goes between the market and the Kpalimé bus stop. House number 86. Find a place where no one will notice you and let me know the minute he goes in or out. If he's going out see if you can follow him but don't take any risks.

— How will I know it's him?

— He's short and fat and pleased with himself.

Jojo smiled at the description and nodded.

— What if he doesn't show up?

— Wait until I ring you. And thanks, Jojo.

Marius climbed back on the bike and watched Jojo as he drove off. Even the back of his head looked serious and just as well. There was no room for joking around and Marius found himself almost praying that no one else was going to get hurt. He had a sudden image of himself as a manic juggler throwing people around, trying to keep them up in the air.

What was Marc doing? There weren't very many garages in the area he'd marked out. Unless he was wrong about that. He went over the things they'd found out. No. No. He had to believe in his logic. If not they all might as well give up now. Then what about Mibou?

Marius grabbed the bar at the back of the bike as the driver made a sharp U-turn and took the side streets down towards the beach road.

The air freshened as they left the congestion behind and got closer to the sea. Marius relaxed a bit and enjoyed the wind rushing past him. Now that Jojo was on his way to AJ's place he felt better. And he felt good that he'd been able to get the information from Bella. Lucien had thought of other people who were likely to be able to tell him the same things about AJ, but the trouble was that Marius didn't know who to trust. That wasn't a problem with Bella so on that score he felt easy. He had confidence in Jojo. Now if only Marc would ring.

There he was again. Checking his watch. Annoying. But yes. He would have time to stop off and check the Rue des Ibis before meeting Gabriel. Everything depended on whether Gabriel was still okay with the plan. In principle he was – last time they'd talked anyway – and Gabriel had never let him down yet.

— Turn here, he told the driver then directed him to the fan palm in the Rue des Ibis.

Marius felt that if he were right about the broken bottle he would be right about the other things. It was a test he was putting himself through as much as a search for evidence.

The driver pulled the bike into the shade of the palm and sat impassively with the engine running as Marius scrambled awkwardly off the bike. More haste less speed he reminded himself. At first he didn't see anything except dirty sand and rubbish that had collected around the base of the palm. Clearly he needed to be more precise. It's not as if a whole bottle was going to be sticking out of the sand, he told himself. The car would have been about here. He held his hand around about where the passenger's head would have been. Quite a bit lower than when standing, it meant the car could get more screening from the palm. He thought about his own car. So the front tyres would have been around about here. He took a pace forward. And the other wheel – he gauged the width of a car – about here. And there it was. Further away from the wall and the palm than he had imagined but small shards of a beer bottle were still lying on the road.

Marius took a small, folded envelope from his back pocket and squatted down next to the glass, his elbows resting on this knees. Not very scientific but he didn't have a choice. He mentally shrugged and carefully picked up some of the jagged pieces of glass and put them in the envelope. The gummed strip on the envelope tasted sweet and unpleasant as he licked it and pressed it closed, rubbing the gummed part to make sure it stayed sealed.

As he walked back to the moto-taxi Marius saw the driver watching him. He looked almost interested but still didn't say anything. Just waited for Marius to tell him where to go.

— As if you're going to the university and then a right. I'll let you know.

Marius didn't want to chance going back to the tilapia place. Not with the turn things had taken. Most of the regular places where he went were out for the time being. The Regent was no good. The Cameroonians would be watched he was sure. Definitely not Le Jazz Spot. His house was out. As if he wasn't putting his family at enough risk without meeting Gabriel there. Then he'd remembered the cheerful little spot with the charming name, Joie de Boire. It had cold beer and great goat soup. He'd found it when he was at the uni, tucked away in a lane off a back street. Perfect. And Gabriel knew it too from those days when they'd met there. He had a sudden thought that it mightn't be there any more, then told himself not to worry. The goat soup was too good – it wasn't going to close.

As the driver negotiated the sandy lane Marius felt he'd made a good choice of meeting place. Cascades of purple bougainvillea and drooping clusters of yellow flowers on the cassia trees were enough to make anyone feel better. And this was also an anti-government stronghold – lots of academics and students lived out here – and Tete Senyo and his mob weren't likely to show up.

As he paid the driver Marius looked over his shoulder and saw that Gabriel was there already, looking comfortable. He was sitting at the table on the verandah under the shade of a cassia tree, sipping on a beer.

As Marius pulled out a chair and sat down, the waitress came over to take their order. Once she'd gone, Gabriel went straight to the point.

— I hope you know what you're doing Marius.

— So do I, so do I.

— I'm serious.

— So am I. If it wasn't for Mibou I'd just drop the whole thing. But you know as well as I do that there's no hope for him unless we can pin Louis' murder – and the other murders – on the people responsible. What I want you to do is to help me get a 'confession' so I can force Emmanuel to throw his weight around.

— How sure are you about this musician? What if he's the wrong man?

Marius leaned forward and spoke very quietly.

— I'm as sure as I can be. If there was any legal way to bring him in for questioning I'd do it without hesitating. Remember what our friend Socrates was fond of saying: Nothing is to be preferred before justice.

Maybe he was over-using that, Marius thought, but it was exactly how he felt.

Gabriel mulled it over for a minute then made up his mind and nodded thoughtfully.

— Okay. By the way, have you heard about Paulie? Marius shook his head and leaned back in his chair. So Gabriel had been doing some asking around. That made him feel a lot better.

Gabriel continued.

— People say that he's not the favourite any more. The Crocodile's not happy.

Marius felt a surge of relief.

— So we can go ahead?

— Yes Marius. We can go ahead. But like I said, you'd better be right.

The waitress arrived with steaming bowls of goat soup and fufu and more beer. It was then that Marius' phone rang.

27

In the windowless room at the back of the workshop Marc felt the first prickling of fear. What was going on? The clean-shaven man in the business suit was still standing at the door, only now he was putting the key in his pocket.

Marc hesitated. He thought he'd have a good chance against the man. But what if he had a knife? Or a gun? And if he did try to fight him for the key what of his story of getting a quote? He'd wait. It wasn't hard to act naturally: confused, surprised, frightened and aggrieved. That's how he felt.

— Hey. What's going on?

— You tell me. The man walked over behind the desk and sat down opposite Marc. The worn leather-look plastic chair was on castors and the man pushed it back with one movement of his foot and leaned against the wall, one leg crossed over the other.

— I came here to get a quote to have my car painted, the guy outside tells me the boss does all the quotes, he brings me in here and the next thing I know, you're locking me in your office.

The man rested his chin on his folded hands and looked at Marc without saying anything.

If he was doing it to unnerve Marc, then it was working. Marc felt confused. How much did this man know? The image of the sticker on the bumper bar was so clear in his mind he had the crazy idea that maybe the man was reading

224

his thoughts! Should he say nothing and wait for the man to speak? But wouldn't that make him look suspicious? Marc couldn't think of anything he'd done to attract this sort of attention and thought he might still have a chance to make the man believe his story.

— What else would I be doing? What sort of a place is this anyway? Then he stood up and went over to the door. He turned the handle. It was definitely locked. Unlock this door for me. I'll get my car done somewhere else. He thought he didn't do such a bad job of sounding innocent and outraged.

— Don't be silly. Sit down. Let's have a chat.

Marc didn't move from the door.

— Okay. Stand if you must, the man said. That's just it you see. We're not sure that's what you really want.

— Like I say, what else would I be doing?

— You've heard of the talking drums I presume? They tell me you're looking for something other than a paint job. Same story in all the places. Same nosey sniffing around the yards. We think you're working for somebody who wants to make trouble for us. And we don't like it.

The man had spoken in a lazy drawl in educated French. Marc was sure this was more than just a workshop for repairing cars. He was still standing beside the door and felt awkward.

— What's your name? The man asked.

Marc wasn't sure he should give him his name but he didn't have another one ready and he blurted it out.

— Marc. And you are?

The man shot up out of the chair and in a flash had Marc by the front of his shirt and was pushing his head back against the door.

— None of your business. Now tell me what you're really doing here.

Marc was finding it hard to breathe but he choked out the words.

— I just want a quote for my car.

The next thing he knew he was falling backwards. There was no way he could break the fall; there was nothing to hold on to. He grabbed at the chair but it slid sideways. A sickening pain shot through the back of his nose as his head hit the edge of the table, and for a minute or two he was unconscious. When he came round it was an effort to work out where he was and he had no idea how long he'd been out to it. Not very long he guessed. He could hear the man talking and realised he was on his mobile.

— You better come down and take the car. It's finished anyway – just a bit of tidying up to do. I told you to dump it at the start. You can talk to him. Says he's just getting a quote but he's been snooping around. We'll have to get rid of him now.

Marc turned over on his side and tried to push himself up, but his legs weren't responding and his head was throbbing. He'd missed his chance. The man let himself out the door and locked it behind him. He heard the noise of a car coming into the workshop then the squeak of unoiled metal and a couple of sharp bangs. The workshop door closing.

At least he'd found the car. Must ring Marius. He reached into his shirt pocket for his phone. Not there. Then in panic and knowing it wasn't there, in his other pockets. The man must have taken it while he was out to it. Of course. Shit. What a mess.

He sat for a while on the floor, his head against his knees. The person the man was talking to must be AJ, Marc guessed. Sounded like he'd be coming here soon.

Using the table as support, Marc pulled himself upright and stood still while the throbbing in his head eased. He screwed up his face and tentatively felt the back of his head with his hand. A big lump had already formed. He looked at his hand. There was blood on it but not too much. He looked around for something to wipe his hand on and spotted some old rags in the mess on the filing cabinet. It took a bit of rubbing to get all the blood off and as he did it Marc looked at the pile of old car parts and broken tools. At least there were plenty of things he could use as a weapon. He threw the cloth back on the pile and picked through the tools. What he needed was something that he could hold in his hand or put in his pocket without it being noticed. But it had to be really hard – something like a knuckle-duster. Now that Marc knew he'd have to fight his way out he felt strangely better. This time he'd be prepared.

He found just what he was looking for. It wasn't obvious to him what it had been part of originally but now the broken part made a handle and the heavy metal sat pretty well on top of his hand. If he made his move when they were coming in the door he stood a good chance of getting away. The karate he'd learned would be useful too. It was three or four years since he'd done any, but perhaps it would come back when he needed it.

There was the noisy rasp of the door being rolled up and Marc heard voices. The boss and another man. Not a voice he recognised so not the shifter man. Must be AJ. They were speaking French. The new voice had a strong Kabyé accent and an arrogant, complaining tone. Marc stood next to the wall. When the door opened, he'd be hidden behind it. He pressed his ear against the wall. The two men were arguing.

— The thing is, I don't know anyone called Marc. No idea what he'd be doing here. He was probably just getting a quote for his car like he said. Is it the red one out there? Could do with a paint job.

Then the boss. Implacable. Smooth.

— I want you to talk to him. You might recognise him. Marc mightn't be his real name.

— Leave me out of it. I'll take the car. Park it out of the way behind my house. Are the keys in it?

— What you're going to do, AJ, is to come into that office with me and eyeball the guy who calls himself Marc. I've asked Ajoii to take care of him but before he gets here I want to know more about what he was doing here. It's not going to hurt you to have a look.

— I've got problems with enough people. I don't want any more. Where's it going to stop?

— Going soft?

— I just don't want trouble.

There was silence for a while. What was going on? Maybe they'd gone back outside. Then the whining voice of AJ again.

— It's my car. I won't be treated like this.

— You're a piece of shit. Scared of your own grandmother. Why the fuck did Ajoii ever get you involved? This way.

The voices were coming towards the office. Marc gripped the chunk of metal in his right hand and waited.

AJ was still complaining about being forced against his will but Marc didn't really hear. He was focused on his attack.

The key turned in the lock and the door opened slowly.

Wait until they're in the room, Marc told himself. Wait.

He could feel the way the boss went into alert mode when he didn't see him. But he kept coming in to the office. He hadn't worked out yet where Marc was.

— You can stop playing games. He raised his voice for the first time. There's someone here who wants to talk to you.

As he was hoping, the boss seemed sure Marc was behind the desk and he went towards it. AJ followed, keeping well back.

Marc sprang. He lashed out with his right hand and his left leg and knocked AJ sideways.

He was out the door. No point closing it, the boss still had the key. Marc headed for the shoulder-high gap in the roller door, dodging between the cars and piles of junk.

He ducked his head as he raced through the door. Behind

him he could hear the two men in pursuit and the boss yelling something in Kabyé.

He saw his car where he'd left it and raced past. He was going to make it. Once in the street they wouldn't dare touch him.

Then the gates closed in front of him with a thud. Damn. It must be the man with the shifter. Where was he?

The gate was made of metal with diagonal struts supporting the inside. Marc grabbed the top of the gate and jammed his right foot against the strut.

Then everything went black.

The man bent over and looked at Marc, the heavy shifter still in his hand. Marc was spread out on his back where he'd fallen and this time he wasn't moving.

AJ and the boss came up to him and the three of them peered down at Marc.

The boss was first to speak.

— Quick thinking Atsu. Then he turned to AJ. Take a leg each. Looks like the trunk of your car again AJ.

The fight had gone out of AJ. He wasn't even complaining. It only took a couple of minutes for the two of them to get Marc into the boot of the BMW.

— The car has to stay until Ajoii gets here. What's keeping him? The boss pressed the button to relock the car. He wasn't happy. Let's get the hell out of here. Ajoii can meet us at the Bar X. You'd better come with us, he said to Atsu. We might need you later. But get that door closed first.

28

Friday 26 March

Gabriel drove and Marius directed him. There were no names on any of these dirty little streets and one looked very much like the other. Two blocks in from the tyre repair place Jojo had said. What was a block? It was impossible to get up much speed. Marius struggled with the desperate feeling that they might not find it in time.

Then he saw the Bar X on the corner. They were getting close.

— Turn here.

Gabriel pulled the car into yet another ugly little street and suddenly they were there. It was a sandy lane that joined two streets. They'd driven past a minute ago and missed it but now Marius could see his old brown Toyota at the other end, parked close against a pile of grey concrete blocks.

As they turned into the lane they saw three men. One man in greasy shorts was reaching up, putting a padlock through a thick metal chain that was wrapped around the top of a closed gate. Another man in a business suit and a short stocky man in jeans and a dark blue polo shirt were watching. All three froze when they saw the little blue and white police car. Like animals caught in the headlights.

— That's them, Marius said. AJ's the one in blue. Thanks Jojo he said to himself.

— Three of them! Let's hope they're not carrying. I'm calling for back up anyway.

Gabriel spoke into the car radio.

— Don't forget the tow truck, Marius reminded him.

Gabriel added a request for a tow truck and pulled the police car up close to the three men. They were still standing there as if paralysed. When he turned off the engine they seemed to come to their senses. Gabriel was out of the car fast but not fast enough for the man in blue. Suddenly he turned and ran.

— Stop or I'll shoot. Gabriel had his handgun out and was pointing it at the running figure.

AJ kept running. Gabriel didn't want to be bothered chasing this idiot. He guessed he would scare easily and fired a couple of shots in the air. It sounded deafening in the narrow street and AJ stopped and turned around.

Behind him a blue and white covered police truck turned into the other end of the lane.

AJ looked ridiculous, like a scared rabbit.

Good timing, Marius thought. Mibou was right; this bad bassist was not very sharp. But on the whole he was glad that AJ had run like that. At least there was no doubt that he was guilty of something and that meant he was on the right track. Reassuring. Marius didn't want to think how bad he'd look if he'd got it all wrong.

The others had stood their ground and Gabriel turned his back on AJ and went over to them. Marius joined him.

The man in the suit was making a show of innocent cooperation.

— What's all this about?

Gabriel had seen a lot of his type and wasn't taken in. He ignored him. There was something wrong about the dark suit in a place like this.

— Hands against the car.

The officers from the police truck came up to Gabriel. Two of them were either side of AJ, each gripping an arm.

— What should we do with this loser?

— Cuff him and hang on to him for the time being. Gabriel turned to the second policeman. And you can search this guy.

Marius watched as one of the policemen handcuffed AJ's hands behind his back. The other officer expertly relieved the man in the suit of keys, phones, wallet, bits and pieces. He passed the wallet to Gabriel who opened it and carefully selected a driving licence from among the cards in the middle fold.

Gabriel motioned to the policeman to let the man move away from the car.

— So, he said, reading from the licence: Mr Bossou. This your place? Gabriel waved his hand in the direction of the locked gates.

— That's right. It's my workshop. What right do you have to stop me like this? I demand that my things are returned immediately.

— What sort of workshop?

— Like it says: Auto-repair. He pointed to the faded sign painted on the fence. Repairing cars. Paint jobs. That sort of thing.

— So you wouldn't mind if we have a look in the premises?

— Why would you want to do that? You can see we've just locked up.

— Who's this friend of yours?

— Not a friend. A customer.

Gabriel turned to AJ. He was squirming under the grip of the policemen. When he heard what Bossou said he started to say something then stopped.

— Your name? Gabriel snapped.

— Abéyobjoli Jouriass.

— Occupation?

— Entrepreneur.

— So you have a car in there? Gabriel nodded at the gates, which were still locked.

— Yes. Is that against the law? AJ sounded pathetic, like a petulant child.

Marius was thinking it was time to get in to the car yard. Where was Marc? Come on Gabriel.

— No. But we have reason to believe your car may have been used unlawfully. Gabriel turned to the man in shorts and ordered him to unlock the gates.

The man was used to following orders and after a minute or two the gates swung open. Gabriel motioned for the others to go first and he and Marius followed. The two policemen were still holding AJ between them and although he was a few paces behind them Marius could see the way AJ stiffened as they drew near to the roller doors. For a second it seemed as if he was going try to make a run for it again, but the policemen tightened their grip.

The yard went alongside the building and around the back. While the roller doors were being unlocked and opened Marius strolled through the cars that were parked there. There were a couple of Audis, a Mercedes and a Saab, all in various stages of being repainted. Strips of masking tape held newspaper over the windows and the cars looked strangely naked without their bumper bars.

As Marius came back towards the workshop he squeezed between the Saab and the corrugated iron fence and had to climb around the discarded bumper bars that were piled up in a heap. He was looking around to see where he could put his foot when he almost stepped on it. For a bumper sticker it was big. The letters G i b s o n were heavy, black, angular, and sloping to the left; they were stylised so that the 'b' looked like an 'l' and the 'n' looked like a 'y'. The black was highlighted with an iridescent orange that shaded into hectic red. Underneath Gibson were the letters USA. These were a light blue.

He heard the sound of the roller door going up and went over to where the others were standing in front of a dark coloured car that was parked just inside the entrance to the workshop. The contrast between the bright sun and the darkness of the workshop made it hard to see anything at first. Then someone flipped the light switch.

For a second Marius was thrown by the deep green of the car, then he saw the blue and white in the black circle and the letters BMW. The serial number didn't mean much to him but at least it started with a three. It was the only BMW here and was missing its bumper bar – no time to do any checking, he'd just have to go with his hunch.

Gabriel turned to Marius, sounding very official.

— Would you say this is the car we've been looking for? Gabriel asked.

Marius matched Gabriel's official tone. He was here as a special officer and needed to sound like one.

— This is the car alright. Bring the owner in for questioning.

Gabriel turned to AJ.

— That your car? He asked.

AJ's eyes looked big with fear. There was no point in lying, but he didn't say anything, just nodded.

— Right. Like the officer said, you're coming with us for questioning in relation to four counts of murder. You and your car.

AJ's eyes got even bigger but he kept his mouth shut.

— Now, just tell us the whereabouts of the young man by the name of Marc and we'll go. Gabriel spoke to all three. None of them said anything so Gabriel continued. He was here earlier today. Tall, athletic. Drives that red Opel over there.

Marius was watching Bossou carefully. Very apt name he thought. The face was hard to read but he was squaring his shoulders as if ready for a fight.

— You've got your man and your car. Take them away and leave us in peace. I can't vouch for every customer who wants a car painted. I demand to have my things back.

Gabriel ignored him and walked between the car bodies and junk up to the office. He looked around then came back.

— No one there, he said to Marius. Are you sure he's here?

— Has to be. Just has to be. Then Marius remembered something that had been just outside his conscious mind. Something he'd heard that wasn't right. It was the phones. The boss had two phones. Why? Because one belonged to someone else. Marc? No wonder he wasn't answering his phone.

Marius took out his phone and called Marc's number. The policeman had taken it off Bossou and stashed it with the other things in a plastic bag and put it in his pocket. Now he took it out and looked at it.

— Marc's phone, Marius told them. I just rang it. So, Mr Bossou, you've never seen Marc.

Bossou was a dark-skinned man but Marius sensed a dark shadow pass over his face.

— You'll regret this, he threatened. You have no idea how much.

Marius privately thought he might but he ignored the comment and looked around the workshop. If Marc wasn't in the office then he'd have to be in a car; that's all there was here, inside and out. Then he looked at the BMW and thought about Louis.

He walked along the side of the car, using one hand to shield his eyes as he peered through the windows. Then he tried the button that opened the trunk. Locked.

— We need the keys to this car. He turned to the policeman who'd just produced the phone. They're probably in the same place as the phone.

The policeman got the bag out of his pocket again and produced some car keys. He went over and tried them in the boot of the BMW and there was a click as the locks popped up.

Marius was afraid of what he might find. Gabriel came over to join him as he opened the trunk.

— Marc!

He was almost doubled up in the cramped space, his back facing them. Gabriel leaned into the trunk and felt for a pulse.

— He's alive.

Marius realised that was more than he'd been expecting and he started to breathe again. Marc was unconscious and very hot. No wonder. Locked up in this workshop in the heat of the afternoon.

Gabriel called an ambulance then put his phone back in his pocket and turned to Marius.

— Let's take him out where he can get some air. Help me support his head. He called over to the policeman who had unlocked the car. Can you come and take his legs.

As carefully as they could the three of them pulled Marc out of the trunk and carried him outside. The concrete was hard but it was shaded by the building so they lowered him gently on to it. Gabriel knelt down beside him and did a quick safety check then rolled him on to his back.

Marius squatted down on the other side and leaned closer.

— Marc. Can you hear me?

Then he noticed something coming from Marc's ear. He looked on the other side. It was the same. Blood.

Marius had no clear idea what that meant but he was sure it was serious and he felt sick with worry. Gabriel had seen it too and he was folding a handkerchief to make a soft pad that he put against the side of Marc's head.

— He's bleeding from a wound on this side of his head, Gabriel said. I can't see what sort of mess they've made but with the blood coming out his ears it could be a compound fracture or worse. At least he's not dead. Another few hours and he would have been.

He handed over the job of staunching the blood to one of the policemen then stood up. Marius stood up as well and spoke quietly so only Gabriel could hear him.

— I've been thinking it might be better if we send Marc to Alain's place. Marius was referring to a mutual friend of theirs who ran a private hospital in Lomé. What do you think? He'd be safer there.

— Good idea. It seems pretty obvious that we've stirred up a hornets' nest and the big players are still out there. God knows we don't want anything else to happen to Marc. He'll be fighting to pull through as it is and he'll get better treatment there as well.

Marius gave Alain a ring. He kept it as brief as possible but explained about the head injury and the need for security. Alain didn't seem too surprised and promised to look after Marc. Relieved, Marius walked over to where Gabriel was talking to the policemen. They'd taken the initiative and handcuffed all three men. None of them looked pleased at the turn of events but AJ looked the worst.

— Right, Gabriel said. So let's hear how this man comes to be locked in this car with his head smashed in.

No one said anything. Marius could see that AJ was looking at Bossou, probably expecting him to say something. But the man in the suit said nothing.

— And yet, Gabriel said, here we have Marc in the trunk of a BMW in this workshop. Are you telling us that he climbed in there by himself and because he liked it so much he decided to lock himself in there and take a nap?

— It's his car. Bossou pointed to AJ. How would I know what's in the trunk?

AJ looked at Bossou as if he was going to explode with indignation.

— It's been here for a week. You tell me why that man's in the trunk.

It was a stand off.

The wah-wah of a siren broke into the uneasy silence, getting closer and louder until an ambulance pulled up inside the gate. The shrill noise suddenly stopped and the silence was reconfigured.

Paramedics expertly loaded Marc into the back of the ambulance. Marius explained to the driver the quickest way to Alain's hospital. The ambulance left. Marius phoned Alain.

— He's on his way. Head wound. Looks bad.

Satisfied that at least Marc was in good hands, Marius left Gabriel and the policemen and strolled up the lane to where Jojo was still waiting in the Toyota, listening to the radio. Marius opened the passenger door and sat down.

— My friend. Thank you. There'd be more to talk about later but right now that was as much as he could manage.

— Is Marc okay? Jojo asked.

— He's alive. Looks like a bad head wound but he's young and fit and we've sent him to Alain's hospital so I think he'll pull through. You can go home now – I'll see you back there.

When Marius got back to the workshop the tow truck had arrived and the BMW was loaded on to the back.

They headed off in convoy, the two police vehicles and the tow truck. Marius looked back as they turned out of the ugly little lane and hoped that was the last he'd see of it.

29

The convoy split up before the border. Gabriel and Marius hadn't counted on having three 'arrests'. They needed to get AJ by himself. But now Bossou and his offsider had to be kept quiet too. It was clear that Bossou thought himself above the law, which to Marius meant one thing: he had powerful friends.

It was Brutus who'd helped Marius to make a guess at who those people were. Brutus, friend of AJ and a lackey of Paulie, the President's brother. That meant they were likely to be very powerful indeed and Marius was worried about who else knew what was going on. When they'd arrived at the car yard the men had been about to leave. What did that mean? Were they planning to leave Marc in the car overnight? Maybe. But maybe they were waiting for someone else to arrive. And if that was the case, when that person arrived and got wind of the situation what was going to happen? He'd find out that Bossou and Atsu had been taken away by the police and if they all had the backing of the President then the shit would hit the fan. But Marius was counting on the fact that Paulie was acting without the knowledge of the President; that was a very different scenario.

Thank goodness Gabriel understood the situation. He sent the two policemen with Bossou and Atsu to the station headquarters. AJ was transferred from the van to Gabriel's car, the other two were going to be locked up in the holding room behind his office at the border police headquarters. No charges were to be laid. Not yet. Above all, it was vital that Major Senyo didn't get wind of what they were doing. He was probably the person who could do the most damage in the shortest time.

Gabriel had chosen the Lomé side of the border between Togo and Ghana as the place to confront AJ. That was his domain; the gendarmes rarely made an appearance, and the military only when they were closing the border.

It was an ugly, dirty, menacing place that had turned its back on the turquoise sea that was obscured by the overloaded trucks and straggling buildings. Anything could happen here; anyone could fall victim.

There was always a long line of trucks, a few cars, and a constant stream of people crossing on foot. The border had been drawn straight through Ewé land and families ended up on either side. Children even crossed the border to go to school. Mostly people negotiated the barriers and gates without papers and without a problem but occasionally someone would be singled out and taken off.

When that happened they were taken to a room to be beaten, questioned, locked up, intimidated. That was the room that Gabriel had decided to use to put some pressure on AJ.

It was in a faded blue concrete building. On a narrow verandah outside, immigration officers were processing truck drivers and travellers who had formal papers to present, or needed an entry visa into Togo. From a barred window to the right a customs officer wielded the final stamp. The room was behind there.

No one took any notice of them as they hustled AJ up the stairs and into the room. It was safer not to notice such things.

When Gabriel flicked the light switch a naked bulb gave out a dull yellow light that did nothing to improve the stained cement walls and floor. The room was claustrophobic and hot. A shaky looking wooden table and some dirty plastic chairs had been put there for Gabriel and the others.

The plan was to intimidate AJ and it was working even before they asked a single question.

Marius could feel AJ's panic. Just what he was planning. Provided those other two were kept isolated, it shouldn't be too hard. AJ need never know how unofficial this all was. Gabriel was wearing a khaki cotton uniform and a green beret. Marius had wondered what to wear and consulted Eva. She'd come up with the idea of camouflage gear and Jojo had picked up some pants and a matching shirt in the markets, plus a wide black leather belt. Gabriel had decided Marius should be a lieutenant. Lieutenant Lumo.

What AJ saw were two uniformed police officers. Gabriel pushed AJ into a chair and he and Marius sat on the other side of the table. A battery operated cassette recorder and a dog-eared notebook were the only things on the table.

Gabriel checked the tape and there was an official sounding click as he pushed the record button. He let it run for a few seconds, said testing a few times then rewound it and played it back. Good. It worked.

— 26 March 2004. 1530 hours. Captain Eshun and Lieutenant Lumo interviewing suspect Abéyobjoli Jouriass. Go ahead Lieutenant Lumo – you have some questions to ask.

— So, Jouriass. You are the owner of a series 3 BMW – Marius checked his notebook –precisely, a 3.18 sedan.

— You know I am. But I know nothing about that man in the trunk. You've got the wrong person.

— We're not here to talk that. Were you driving that BMW on 13 March?

— How would I know?

— Think about it. Not last Saturday but the one before that. A lot happened that should help you remember that day.

— Saturday 13 March? AJ made a show of thinking. Ah. I remember now. I was out of town. There was a funeral in Kara.

— You have witnesses?

— There were a lot of people there.

— I'm sure there were. But what we think you were doing is this. You drove your car along a lane leading to Rue des Ibis. Parked behind a palm tree for long enough to shoot into a crowd of peaceful opposition supporters. Killed two of them and seriously injured a third.

— Ridiculous. What lane? What palm? I keep telling you, you've got the wrong man. Let me go!

Marius opened the sports bag he'd brought with him.

— Our forensic team has been doing some work. This is what they found. Exhibit A. Marius pulled out a small plastic bag and held it up. He pointed to the shard of green glass inside it. Tests on this glass show that it came from the same bottle as glass that was removed from the front right tyre of your car. The car was taken to a Tokoin tyre repair workshop on Saturday 13 March.

Marius was guessing. AJ looked less certain but stood his ground.

— What tests? That glass could have come from any street in Lomé.

— But it didn't. Let me tell you what you did next. You wanted to get away from there as fast as you could. You accelerated and turned right into the Rue des Ibis. But then you saw Louis Baradou. Louis had seen you. He'd seen you shooting those people. Louis recognised you, so you pinned him against the wall with your car and shot him. Or forced him into the car at the point of a gun. Or hit him with the gun.

— I tell you. I was in Kara. You're both insane. This is a mad house. Why would I want to kill Louis Baradou?

— You didn't want to kill him. You had to kill him. He'd seen you. What would he do? Who would he tell? You had to get rid of him.

Marius gave AJ credit for his acting. He was shaking his

head, that aggrieved look had come back. Good. He was getting angry. Not for a minute did Marius think it was AJ who'd done the shooting, but it shouldn't take much more before he told them who did. Marius leaned down and pulled out of the bag the plaster mold of the tyre tread. He dropped it onto the table with a bang.

— You can see our forensic team has been busy. Marius smiled to himself thinking of Mimi. Exhibit B. This is a print of your tyre. It was taken from tread marks next to the wall. It's a perfect match with the treads on the tyres on your car and the marks were at the exact point that Louis would have been, according to our witness.

— You're lying. There was no one there. AJ suddenly realised what he'd said. Marius savoured the moment and said nothing. The man's stupidity was stunning.

Gabriel leaned towards AJ, his elbows on the table, chin resting on his folded hands.

— So now, why don't you tell us what really happened. Perhaps there was someone else with you.

AJ took the bait.

— All I did was drive the car. I was forced to, he added as an afterthought. There's this man who threatened me unless I helped him.

— Let's start from the beginning, Gabriel prompted. Helped you do what?

AJ was warming to his story now.

— He told me I had to drive to that lane and pull over. The next thing I knew he was shooting into the rally. Then he said Go! Go! And I went fast. But there was Louis. He'd seen me and this man goes, run him over. But Louis went against the wall so I drove right next to him. This man knocks him out with his gun and shoves him in the back seat.

— And the name of this man?

AJ seemed to realise what he'd just said and sat silent.

Gabriel suddenly stood up and hit the table with his clenched fist.

— The name! If you want to get out of here, tell me the name!

AJ wasn't the heroic type. He was a puffed up toad; a straw man. Since Lucien and Bella had told him about AJ, Marius had developed his own profile of this bad bassist. This was him: inflated with a sense of his own importance. A weakling who did favours for unscrupulous men to make himself feel tough. A selfish man who put himself before everything and everyone.

— Ajoii. His name is Ajoii Doussou.

Gabriel sat down and picked up his pen and Marius took over again.

— And this Doussou. He thought nothing of killing a few innocent people. Then he knocked Louis out and drove him – let me guess. Not to your house. Not to his own house. A big place where no one would take any notice if a few shots were heard.

Marius had been thinking aloud. Then suddenly he knew as surely as if he'd been told. Paulie's. It had to be Paulie's house.

— Let's say this place has a security wall decorated with mosaics and that it's next to the Presidential Palace. Marius was describing what he knew of Paulie's mansion. Did you scare the horses?

Paulie was well known for playing polo. An unsettling sight, the huge man on the little pony.

— Perhaps Major Senyo was there too, Marius continued, inspired now. And this Doussou, the hit man. He shot Louis. And you….

In the back of AJ's eyes Marius saw a flicker of real fear. Or maybe it was hatred. Or both. Whatever it was, it was too much. AJ struggled with the handcuffs and thrust out his fat chest, eyes popping. Suddenly he was on his feet, yelling at Gabriel and Marius.

— You think you're so smart. What if a few people are dead? You're just policemen. You're nothing.

Gabriel had been writing in the record of interview book. He ignored AJ and spoke to Marius.

— Ten more minutes. Then we'll have to go.

— Right. Marius turned back to AJ who had sat down again. So, Doussou shot Louis at this place we're talking about.

— What of it? You're going to end up dead too. Just wait.

— That's a yes?

AJ gave the faintest of nods with his head. Gabriel wrote it down.

Marius leaned forward and stared at AJ.

— Then the next time someone sees your car, it's the early hours of Sunday morning and you're driving through Agkamé with your lights off. Louis' body's found on the beach in the morning. But it's not enough that you dump him there and mutilate him. You have to shoot another innocent man as well. All he's doing is taking a leak. Why AJ? Why shoot him?

— All I did was drive. Ajoii was the one who did the....I just helped drag the body onto the beach. They told me to get back in the car.

— So there was a third person with you. Makes sense. The shot had to come from the driver's side. And that person shot Kodjo. AJ looked surprised and Marius explained. He has a name, you know. They all have names because they're real people. Who was with you?

AJ said nothing. Marius used the time to think. On Sunday there'd been that weird episode with the snake. Then it fell into place.

— I'm going to make a guess. The person who went along for the ride and helped drag Louis from the car to the beach was Bruno. AJ couldn't stop himself from looking surprised.

Marius felt triumphant. To paraphrase Socrates, AJ, an honest man is always a child. But don't be fooled. I might be nothing. And who knows? Perhaps your friends might win in the end. But it worries me. It upsets me that people die and no one cares. I care and now I know something. It was Bruno who shot Kodjo.

— He was plastered, AJ said scornfully. Ajoii put his gun on the back seat while we were at the beach. Bruno was playing around with it and fired out the window just as we were getting to those shanties. Stupid.

As if he was shooting an animal. Marius suddenly felt tired and profoundly sad.

— Maybe it's not too late for you AJ. The judge might be lenient if you assist the enquiry and show remorse. I don't think you're a killer, but you may as well be one.

That was enough. He had what he needed. Now he had to act.

Gabriel read back an account of the 'interview' and made AJ sign it. He switched off the recorder and took out the tape.

They marched AJ out of the room and back into the car.

Marius could see Gabriel was worried. What was happening back at headquarters? Were the other two still safely locked up? Someone would come looking for them eventually and then who knew what would happen unless they kept a move ahead.

Now they really needed the help of Emmanuel, a judge of the Supreme Court and Selina and Eva's cousin. With all the evidence he had, Marius felt fairly sure Mani would listen and act. Heaven help them all if he didn't.

30

Marius left Gabriel at the border police headquarters. AJ was locked up with Bossou and Atsu in the holding cell. No one had asked about them yet but Marius knew there was someone pulling the strings and it wouldn't be too long before things started to happen. He was counting on at least a day and by that time it would be out of his hands.

Sitting on the back of a moto-taxi, Marius went over the day. He checked his watch. 5.30. Mani should be home by now. If Eva had got through to him, he would be expecting Marius. The day hadn't quite gone to plan but near enough. He wasn't looking forward to having to tell Eva about Marc, but at least Alain thought he should make a full recovery. Phew. Marius wasn't going to forget the sight of Marc in the boot of that car in a hurry. He didn't need anyone to tell him what a dangerous position he'd put Marc in. Would he do it again? Hard to say.

What Alain had told him was that the fracture was compound but not severe and there was no need for an operation. He'd be in intensive care for a few days but then he should be fine. No danger of brain damage. What about Edith? He gave her a ring. It was hard to hear with the noise of the bike and the traffic but she sounded okay. Still speaking to him.

Mani's house was in a pretty tree-lined street in La Caisse, a residential area that was like an oasis in the straggling untidiness of the rest of Lomé. Marius was buzzed in the gates and when he knocked on the front door of the tasteful big house it was Mani himself who opened it, obviously expecting him. That was a good start.

Marius had thoughts about the compromises you'd have to make to be a judge of the Supreme Court in Togo but he always kept them to himself. Mani looked as if he was thriving on it. The casual shirt and trousers looked French and expensive. And, Marius had to admit, stylish. Pragmatism and quick wits had got Mani to where he was. Connections too of course. But he was fundamentally a good person trying to do the best he could in a corrupt system.

Mani looked at Marius then stepped back and looked again.

— Good god man. What are you wearing? I didn't recognise you at first.

Marius looked down at his clothes and threw his head back and laughed. He was still wearing his camouflage outfit. No wonder the moto driver had been so polite.

— Eva's idea, he said. You'll understand when I tell you what I've been doing.

— Speaking of Eva, she said that what you wanted to talk about was serious and urgent. Sounds like it calls for a Glenfiddich. Come through.

Mani's study had a wall of glass looking over a fern-fringed goldfish pond and a carefully tended tropical garden. The room was huge, with an elaborate well stocked bar at the far end. In front of the bar was a small round glass table and two soft leather chairs. Mani waved Marius into one of the chairs then he took a bottle of Glenfiddich and two glasses and put them on the table.

— Ice? Water? Soda?

Marius had already filled the whisky tumbler. He shook his head.

— Thanks.

Mani sat down and poured himself a glass.

— Your health.

— Santé. Marius felt the whisky burning his insides. Hang on to yourself, he thought.

— Serious and urgent, Mani said in his almost flawless French. Let's have it.

It took Marius three glasses of whisky to fill Mani in on the background. The steps they'd taken. The evidence they'd put together, AJ's confession.

From time to time Mani asked questions but mostly he let Marius speak. When Marius had finished, the plaster mold, the glass and the tape were sitting incongruously on the little glass table.

Mani picked up the tape and put it in the stereo system that was set into a cabinet to the right of the bar. Listening to his own voice modified by the Bang and Olufsen speakers gave Marius a surreal feeling. Mani leaned back in his chair with his eyes half closed and listened without comment. When the tape ended Mani sat quietly for a minute, absentmindedly rubbing the tips of his fingers together. It gave Marius no clue to what he was thinking; everything now depended on this man.

Marius realised he'd probably had enough to drink, but he poured himself another small whisky anyway, and relaxed back in the chair. He'd put his pieces in place and there was nothing more that he could do.

— I'm impressed with the way you've managed to put all this together, Mani said. Well done. But you've opened a very smelly can of worms.

Marius felt some of the tension dropping from his neck and shoulders.

— Yes. We got more than we bargained for. By the time we realised it was tied up with politics it was too late to back out. I don't mind telling you that it's a relief to get to this stage. Good of you to hear me out. Do you think there's something you can do?

— The first thing is order an autopsy to be done on the body of Louis. There are people I know who'll do it more or less straight away.

Marius mentally high fived himself. Finally.

— Then, assuming that the results fit with your evidence, I think it's best to meet with the President. And maybe the Justice Minister as well.

— Does that mean you think Paulie's behind the shootings? Marius asked.

Mani got up and walked across to the glass wall. He stood for a minute with his back to Marius, looking out over the garden, then he seemed to make a decision and sat down again.

— Yes. From what you've been able to find out, I'm sure that Paulie is at the back of the shootings. He and Tete Senyo. For some of us it's no secret that Paulie's becoming more than a liability to the government. He's becoming a threat. It seems he's in the hands of this Major Senyo who's plotting to set up Paulie as the next President. My bet is that Paulie wouldn't last long and Senyo would make himself President sooner rather than later.

— So Gabriel should keep AJ and his mates in the lock up?

Mani nodded slowly.

— Absolutely. The last thing I want is for any hint of what I'm doing to get out. I'll give Gabriel a ring – can you give me his number?

Marius pulled out his phone and read out Gabriel's number. He felt as if another weight was dropping off him.

— Do you need me to hang around? he asked Mani.

— No, you go. Mani pointed to the table and the things on it. Leave these. I'm sure Dzigi and Eva want to see you back safe. And change those ridiculous clothes!

31

Marius was doing all the talking.

They were in Le Jazz Spot. A couple of tables had been pulled together close to the bar. It was too late for flies and too early for mosquitoes. The sun was an orange ball in the haze of late afternoon and the sound of Thelonius Monk carefully choosing his notes wafted from the speakers.

No other customers were there and Akosua was treating them like royalty, half listening but hurrying off to get more drinks before any of them had to ask.

Takashi and Mimi had left Chez Miki in the hands of Yao and came in as soon as they got the call from Marius. He'd picked up Lucien on his way to the Spot. Gabriel was sitting next to Marius, definitely off-duty and getting on with Mimi as if they were old friends.

Between Marius and Lucien was Mibou.

He'd spent at least half an hour in the shower, washing and soaping, washing and soaping, over and over again, but he couldn't seem to get rid of the smell of jail. Takashi thought he looked different; subdued, almost frail. And he'd hardly touched his first beer. But he had his saxophone with him. It was still in its leather case on the ground next to the chair and Takashi noticed that Mibou kept touching it as if to make sure it was still there. It had only been a few days since they'd been together at Chez Miki but it felt like weeks.

— And that was how we got AJ to talk, Marius was saying. That evidence was enough for cousin Emmanuel. Mani. He's the one I told you about, a judge of the Supreme Court. I was pretty nervous when I was telling him what we'd found out. Had no real idea if he'd just tell me to forget about it and go home. Thank goodness it coincided with his own interests and he was on to it straight away. Later during the night there was a knock on the door. I thought they'd come for me! Marius couldn't resist a dramatic pause. But it was Mani's driver. He'd brought over a copy of the autopsy report. And we were right! There were three gunshot wounds; the first one probably killed him instantly. He didn't want to think about the other disturbing details.

— So the machete was used to cover up the gunshots – make it look convincing. Takashi spelled it out. It wasn't a question; that was what they'd been convinced of from the start.

— Exactly. But let me go back a bit, there's something I meant to tell you. This hit man, Ajoii. The one who shot Louis and the people in the march. He's the one who was going to 'take care of Marc' – not exactly in the way we would have wanted. Marius tried to make light of it, but it was far from being a joke. Anyway, he continued, Gabriel sent a couple of officers to wait for him at the auto-repair workshop and Ajoii ended up in the lock up at the border police headquarters with the others. The thing is, we knew we had to stop word getting out to Paulie and Senyo. They'd get the wind up eventually, but we needed to buy time. By the way, looks like Ajoii wasn't just a hit man; he was training up a group of paramilitaries as part of the planned coup. Mani didn't tell me much about his meeting with the President and the Justice Minister but it must have been quite early on Saturday morning. Apparently Paulie and the major were having a bit of polo practice waiting for Ajoii when the President's own troops picked them up.

— That seems quick, even for the President, Takashi said. Sounds to me as if they were almost ready for it.

— Sure. Mani said it didn't take much to convince him because AJ's confession put Paulie and Senyo squarely in the frame. I had my suspicions that Paulie was plotting something – Gabriel confirmed it yesterday – so imagine how much the President must have known. The thing I didn't guess was that Tingayama was in it too. You know who I mean? Chief judge of the Supreme Court.

— Yeah, Lucien drawled in a monotone. What a star. Corrupt, unscrupulous, devious and disgusting.

— Right. Paulie and Senyo had been using Tingayama to get inconvenient people out of the way. People like Mibou.

Mibou was only half taking it in, but he looked up and smiled, seeming a bit lost. Marius smiled back, happy just to have Mibou sitting here.

— So what Mani showed was how Major Senyo and Tingayama were the ones who had framed Mibou. That was enough to connect the judge with Paulie and the others. As far as the President was concerned those shootings were as good as a declaration of an attempted coup, so they were arrested on that charge.

Mimi was struggling to put it all together. So were the others.

— But how does this fit in with the shootings? Why was this Paulie involved? She asked.

Marius took a long draught from the fresh beer that Akosua had just put in front of him. Then he put his glass on the table and leaned back in his chair, getting his thoughts in order before he started speaking again.

— Okay. The story goes like this. Paulie is the President's brother. He has privileges, but he's not happy. He's full of his own importance and feels as if he's being passed over, treated like an idiot. Then you have Tete Senyo. A major, just like our

President was before he led his first coup. Smarter than him? Probably. Definitely ambitious. Who knows what motivates people. He sees Paulie as a good front man for his own power grab and he grooms Ajoii, who trains a crack paramilitary corps and does his dirty work. And he bribes Judge Tingayama to get legal support. They're just about ready to make a move but looking for an excuse. Then the President seems to go soft on opposition rallies and that's annoying. The government's trying please the European backers, especially the French, so foreign aid keeps coming in. But that's not good for Senyo and Paulie, so they decide to stir things up themselves, knowing it would be blamed on government troops. What they hoped was that shooting a few demonstrators would spark retaliation, fighting, more anti-government protests. Then they would take over the key facilities and declare a coup in the interests of restoring Togo to a real democracy. Of course they had no intention of doing that. Quite the opposite. It would be back to an even more autocratic sort of dictatorship, without even the show of a parliament.

— So Louis got caught up in all of that? Mimi asked.

Marius nodded.

— And Kodjo. And the people at the march. It's just like in your drawing Mimi. The only difference is that they weren't acting for the RPT, they were acting for themselves. But just as they expected, everyone assumed it was a government attack. By the way, do you still have that drawing?

Mimi reached down into her bag and pulled it out.

— That was a breakthrough moment for me, Marius said.

— You want it? Mimi held it up and looked at it. She made a face. It's messy. But you can have it if you like.

Gabriel put his hand on the other side of the drawing to steady it. He hadn't seen it before.

— So it was Bruno and the snake that brought Paulie into the frame? He asked.

— Yep. Marius pointed to the drawing. And as I remember, it was only when we were watching Mimi sketch it out that we realised the RPT connection – or what we took then to be the RPT connection. Before that we were completely in the dark.

Mimi handed Marius the drawing and then looked at him thoughtfully, her face on one side.

— What do you think would have happened if Emmanuel and the President didn't get to know about the coup plot?

Marius thought about it then shook his head.

— Not sure. But Mani would have been in a tight spot. We might have got the autopsy. Not much else. And I might have ended up in that shit hole with Mibou.

— What about that man at the car place? The one who wanted to kill Marc? Takashi asked.

— Bossou and his offsider? We don't know for sure but it looks as if Bossou was getting paid very well to recycle cars that Major Senyo and his men confiscated on some pretext or other. It was a lucrative business – probably helped to raise funds for the coup.

— What's all this about a coup?

The voice seemed to come from the shadows.

It was very French, a little bit husky. They'd all been so intent on what Marius was saying that none of them had noticed her.

— Françoise! Lucien was the first to find his tongue. Thank God you've come to take this troublemaker off our hands.

Mibou suddenly came to life and went over to where she was standing behind Marius. His face was one big smile and he didn't have to say anything. Akosua gave Françoise a big hug and made room for a chair next to Mibou. They all sat down again.

Françoise felt as if she was back home but she wasn't, she reminded herself.

Mibou took out his saxophone and licked the reed. He played a few notes, adjusted the reed and looked around.

This is for Le Noir and the others, he said. Chanson de Prison Civile.